TAROT FOR THE MILLIONS

"For the Millions" Series

TAROT FOR THE MILLIONS

by Sidney Bennett

FOR THE MILLIONS SERIES

SHERBOURNE PRESS, INC.   LOS ANGELES, CALIFORNIA

FOR BILL, WHO TAUGHT ME SO WELL
WHAT WAS CONTAINED IN THE ACE OF CUPS

Acknowledgments

The ability to read the Tarot well does not come overnight. It is a long and arduous process. To become a Reader is basically simple, but to learn the tiny and very important meanings, buried deeply within the cards, is only possible after much dedication and study. This book was written after nearly eighteen years of investigation. The greatest scholars in the field of divination with Tarot cards were queried, their books thoroughly examined for new clues, new thoughts. In presenting this interpretation of the Tarot I have attempted to incorporate all this vast collection of knowledge, gleaned from sources so varied and so separated geographically that to mention them all would require another book. Three people in particular played a very important part in my Tarot education. My deep and sincere thanks go to British scholars Arthur Edward Waite and Wenzell Brown. These men were invaluable in my search for a definition of the Tarot that is clear, graphic, and remarkably original. Thanks go also to Basil Ivan Rakoczi, the foremost authority on gypsy interpretation of the Tarot cards.

It is not possible, here, to cover the gamut of wise seers living in Europe who were the basis of my education in the Tarot. These wonderful gypsies, who furthered my understanding of the ancient symbol-pictures, are, today, still scattered over the European countryside.

A last word of thanks goes to my friends and my family; they so believed in the necessity of a book about Tarot for the millions that they worked with me, for endless months, looking for new ideas, new thoughts, and new interpretations of the cards.

SIDNEY BENNETT

Contents

CHAPTER ONE

What Is the Tarot?

The Tarot is a series of seventy-eight playing cards, decorated with symbol-pictures. Once you have learned to understand the meanings of the cards, you will have the key that unlocks all the mysteries of life.

Impossible you say? Not at all. Many people, just like yourself, have used the great wisdom of the Tarot for many years. The amazing cards have found their way into the lives of such important men as Sir Winston Churchill; way back in history the great kings of France used the Tarot to delve into the mysteries of life and to plan the futures of their country. One of the great minds of our time, Dr. Albert Einstein, never denied the power of the human mind; as a consequence, he studied the Tarot cards to uncover the secrets locked within. In the present, the film personality Vincent Price uses the ancient cards in the presentation of motion pictures to stress the idea that the future can be probed and that, through an understanding of the cards, an individual may overcome the problems of the present. Very recently, Dr. Frank Baxter, a professor at a California university, presented the history and meaning of the Tarot visually on a Sunday television special. Beyond being a method of divination and a key to the future, the Tarot has presented a philosophical challenge to great thinkers, especially to men of science and religion. Author and psychic researcher Aldous Huxley, prior to his death, found new keys into the potentials of the human mind through an exposure to the Tarot cards.

An interesting Tarot story comes from Fran S, a lovely starlet who makes her home in the quiet San Fernando Valley. Always a practical gal, she was the last person to consider "fortune-telling" an answer to a problem. One rainy night, Fran came to visit and to ask my advice about an agreement with an important film company that she was hesitant to enter into. She felt that somehow she was going to have a problem but couldn't quite put her finger on the source. I suggested that she might consult the Tarot cards. She laughed saying that she didn't believe in such things. After awhile, the idea seemed curious enough to give it a try. She took the cards into her hands and shuffled them.

Her spread told me that she would gain much from signing the contract but she must be very careful of a dark man approaching middle age, whose charming witty surface hid a treacherous and deceitful nature.

The cards advised that she wait six days before signing the contract and all would work out well.

Fran decided to challenge the Tarot reading. She signed the contract, and bet me a steak dinner that the message of the cards was just a silly bit of fun. Three days later, the producer of the show in which she was to be cast asked her to fly with him to Mexico City. The invitation pointedly excluded mention of the producer's wife or his three children. The producer, a witty, dark-complexioned man approaching middle age, flew into a rage when Fran refused. He became quite angry, and threatened to take away Fran's chance at the contract. The next morning, the film studio that employed the producer had a meeting of its advisory board. The producer and his project were suspended for financial reasons. But another producer, who had also seen Fran's screen test and now knew that she was free of commitment, phoned to ask her if she would do a show with him. Two days passed and the contracts between Fran and the producer were signed. Today, Fran has the starring role in a well-known TV series. The portents of the Tarot proved right once again. Incidentally, the steak dinner was excellent.

The Tarot cards have found their way into many lives. When I first met Joyce Greene, she was a quiet, efficient secretary to the president of a large construction corporation. Joyce's aunt, Lilian, a resident of North

Dakota, had sent her a deck of Tarot cards and a book explaining their meanings as a Christmas gift, thinking that her niece would enjoy the unusual present. Joyce read the book from cover to cover and decided to give the strange deck of colorful pictures a try. The cards depicted her basic qualities. They displayed a picture of the perfect wife and mother. Joyce, single and almost thirty years old, thought of her future as spinsterhood, and found the analysis hard to believe. The cards went on to picture a young man, fair and studious, who would be the bearer of an important message. The last two cards in her spread told of much merriment and dancing and, finally, the last card was that of a happy marriage with two children. Impossible! Unbelievable and out of the question, thought Joyce, as she wound her hair onto rollers and got ready for another evening of television and hemming dresses.

One day the following week, Joyce, up to her ears transcribing dictation, was interrupted by a young man standing in front of her desk. He was very tall and blond, and he held an envelope to be hand-delivered to Mr. Fowler, Joyce's employer. The young man spoke with a slight accent. He explained that he had come to America from Germany to obtain his master's degree in engineering. He was working for a local engineering firm in his spare time to gain experience and to earn money for his education. Joyce thought that the young man was charming. Overcoming her usual shyness, she smiled at him and struck up a conversation. When the young engineer had left, Joyce remembered the prophecy of the Tarot but decided that the whole matter was just a coincidence . . . until that afternoon at four o'clock when her telephone rang. It was the fair, studious man, bearer of an important message, asking her to have dinner with him. Almost sliding off her chair, Joyce accepted. That was the beginning. Hans turned out to be a fascinating companion and a wonderful dancer. After a delightful relationship that lasted nearly a year, Joyce and Hans became engaged and were married. The last time I spoke with Joyce and Hans they were expecting their second child and were, in truth, living happily ever after. I am sure that, when Joyce thanked Aunt Lilian for the odd Christmas gift and told her about Hans, Aunt Lilian was not the least bit surprised!

The art of reading the Tarot cards is very old. The Tarot is so surrounded by mystery and legend that no one really knows, to this day, where it originally came from. There are many theories and, for every man who has devoted his life to the study of the Tarot, there is a book by someone else trying to prove him wrong. Since the Tarot first came onto the scene—whether from Egypt as some think, or from Chaldea through Israel and then west, or from India or China or from the eastern European gypsies—certain facts do remain definite. The interpretations will vary from author to author, from country to country, and from artist to artist, but there will always be seventy-eight cards and, when you really get down to it, the pictures are always just about the same.

It is easy enough for you to see something one way while I may, and quite accurately at that, see the very same thing in a different way. The art of divination, or seeing into the future, is as individual as that. The tools are the same for all Readers; only the intuition and judgment of the Reader vary. The messages hidden in the cards may come out through many different methods of presentation but what it all boils down to is that the cards speak wisely and truthfully to the student of the Tarot. The life of every man follows a certain pattern and that pattern is spelled out in the cards. Whether rich or poor, black or white, tall or short, fat or skinny, good or evil, man is a child of nature; he is the end result of everything he has ever known, seen, or experienced. We could say that the real story of the Tarot is the story of man! The Tarot looks into a person's soul and answers all his worldly problems. Through the wisdom of the cards, the past, the present, and the future become clear and make sense.

For hundreds of years, many people have been fascinated by the strange Tarot picture-symbols. Yet for many others of us, the Tarot has come into our homes, right under our noses, and probably never been recognized. Once you have examined a pack of Tarot cards, you will see that the playing cards familiar to us today have evolved from Tarot. Once upon a time, the suits —Hearts, Diamonds, Clubs, and Spades—and the valuable King, Queen, and Jack were all Tarot cards. The Hearts were called Cups, the Diamonds were once known as Pentacles or Coins, the Clubs were then called Wands, and the Spades were called Swords. There was a King, Queen, Knight, and also a Page. In time, the Page and the Knight became one card called the Jack. As time passed the first twenty-two cards in the Tarot deck were discarded altogether.

Looking at the history of cards, it would seem that people have always given cards a mystical value. Even today, many people use the regular deck of fifty-two playing cards to foretell the future. An adept Reader realizes that a common bridge deck incorporates all the original seventy-eight Tarot cards and has a knowledge of their meanings; it is not surprising then that such a Reader can see many events to come and can startle his or her audience with the great wisdom locked in the cards.

CHAPTER TWO

Tarot Reading Is for Everyone

No one is immune to the magic of the cards. One day
last year my dog Oscar came running through the
kitchen chased by a gorgeous poodle. The strange dog
surely lived in another neighborhood as he wasn't one of
the local pets. The two animals chased each other
through the house and, in so doing, turned over the old
wooden box on my coffee table in which I keep my own
Tarot cards. All of the cards fell face down with the
exception of the Queen of Pentacles. I called on the
lady next door, the neighborhood clearing house for all
gossip, and asked her if she knew of any new woman
who had moved into the area, possibly an actress or a
writer or someone dark and probably very lovely. She
told me yes, that an actress had rented the old estate a
few blocks away; then my neighbor continued with a
stream of "factual" statements regarding the lady's
clothing, furniture, and latest suitor. I took the poodle
and went to the house I knew had been up for rent. An
exceedingly attractive, dark-haired girl answered the

door, let out a cry of joy, and reached for the poodle, smothering it with kisses. Again, the wisdom of the Tarot can be absolutely startling!

Anyone can use the Tarot cards and obtain amazing results. Their wisdom is by no means limited to movie stars and people who make their living in the arts. Housewives, doctors, insurance salesmen, wire manufacturers, factory workers, salesgirls, animal breeders—all can learn to read them. In times of great unhappiness, the Tarot is a good, dear friend: understanding and full of wise advice.

Dorothy Kelly is a close school-chum of mine, who now lives in Oklahoma City. We grew up together, we were both exposed to the Tarot at the same time, and we found the cards a marvelous method of understanding things that at times just don't make sense. When Dotty's son Tommy was critically injured in an automobile accident, she called me at once. Always believing that things happen for a good reason, I told Dotty that I would read the cards and write to her immediately. Tommy had been so injured that he would never again be able to participate in any sports. Bad news, indeed, for Tommy had been captain of his college football team. The cards showed Tommy's present and future clearly. Oddly enough the Tarot disclosed that Tommy was destined to be a man of letters—definitely a lot to do with writing and dealing with books! The cards advised a change of living quarters and predicted complete recovery from his injury within one year. I wrote to Dotty saying that she might talk to Tommy about changing his classes and perhaps his major. I offered the thought that he move out of the house where he then lived with his parents. Tommy was what we called a "football head." Sports were his only interest, yet he was a very bright boy. Tommy was so disgusted, when he finally left the hospital, that he sank into a deep gloom. Dotty talked him into changing schools so that he would not have to be surrounded by old memories. Perhaps a new door to the future would open. Within three months Tommy adjusted to his new campus so well that he became captain of yet another team. This time, the subject was debate. Within another month, he changed his major to law. All this came as a shock to Dotty who never expected Tommy to be happy again. Completely on his own, Tommy took the future into his hands and altered the established pattern of his life. Dotty had never given her son the advice or the prediction of the cards. He had just refused to listen to her during that gloomy period. Now Tommy is living on campus. He walks well and is on his way to becoming an attorney. According to the Tarot, he will be truly successful.

A few months ago, I attended a party given for a group of newspaper reporters by a very famous actor. The actor, whom we will call John, is a trademark of the movie industry. You have all seen him and surely loved his hundred of portrayals. In his spare time, John collects paintings and is well known for an amazing art collection, a good part of which decorates his home. One picture in particular caught my attention; it was of an old gypsy woman gazing intently at a spread of cards, which lay on the ground of what appeared to be a cave. I asked John if he was interested in card reading and his gray eyes twinkled. He took a deck of common cards from a desk drawer and asked the assembled group of reporters to gather around while he performed for them. Commenting that this was not the talent that he was most noted for, we all laughed and awaited the reading. I shuffled the cards and, as John instructed, made a wish. He spread the cards in front of him. I was told that I would receive an inheritance shortly but that there would be difficulty with it, involving a short dark man. John went on to say that my wish, which incidentally was the publication of an article that had been submitted to an east coast magazine, would come true within two weeks. The cards told of much change, great motion, and perhaps new living quarters. I laughed, knowing that I had no intention of moving. He continued, saying that I would be traveling very shortly, by air, another doubtful happening, and that I would continue my journey by water. He saw a gift of jewelry in my future and much celebrating. All in all, the reading was lovely but even to me, a firm believer in the power of cards, the predictions seemed rather unlikely at the moment.

A week before Christmas, my grandfather passed away, leaving my sister and myself partial heirs to his estate. The attorney involved was a short, dark fellow and not terribly efficient. The family remained in a state of confusion for weeks before things were finally resolved. I had still not heard a word from New York concerning my article and the two weeks had long passed. My husband came to me a few days later saying that he would have to travel to London on business and thought it would be a wonderful opportunity for me to have a vacation from the daily routine of work and family. I was shocked. London. How exciting!

I was somewhere over the North Pole when I remembered John's reading of the cards and, with my faith in the ancient art restored, I settled back to ponder what would happen next. Once in London, our business finished, Bill suggested that we take the ferry from Dover across the English Channel to France and spend a few days sightseeing in Paris. There was the journey by water! Like most husbands, Bill is a birthday and anniversary gift giver, hardly more than that. He is so wrapped up in his business affairs that he never notices things in shop windows or ads in newspapers. I could paint a picture of something I wanted on the bathroom mirror and Bill would see his face right through it, and go on shaving, lost in thought, completely unaware. Passing a quaint shop on the Left Bank in Paris he suddenly noticed an odd ring in the window. Five minutes later, it was on my finger. Certainly not the typical thing for him to do! The rest of this amazing story unfolded upon our return home. A few days later, the postman knocked on the front door with a special delivery letter. It was from the New York magazine! The letter stated that they had written to me weeks ago and the letter had been returned, stamped "No such address." The editor's secretary had made a mistake! The original letter of acceptance had been sent *exactly* two weeks after John had read my cards! We haven't moved but for the most part John was nearly perfect in his reading of the cards. Even the best fortune teller is permitted a small mistake!

The Tarot, for all the mystery and legend surrounding it, is not at all mysterious in the answers it can give. The questions put to the cards are the basic, everyday problems everyone experiences. With the passage of time only the settings have changed. The wise gypsy in her painted caravan; the old man, using the light of an oil lamp in the heart of snowy Russia; the wigged and gowned ladies of the court of Louis XIV in France in the quiet of a parlor; the Arabian mystic in a room filled with silken cushions; the sounds of a wailing Moslem calling his people to prayer; the professor in his firelit library, pondering the meanings locked in the symbols; the housewife and her neighbor reading the future across a coffee table in a New York suburb; the Creole maid in the noisy French Quarter of New Orleans; the actor in his elegant Hollywood home, searching for the future of his career in the Tarot—all these are pages in the Tarot's history.

Everyone is really so much the same. Our problems, our hopes, and dreams differ only with personality and exposure. Your life is recorded in the seventy-eight cards. Your future is there, just for the asking. What is coming? To find the answers, go to the next chapter where we talk about each card, one at a time, and teach you its meaning. Then you will learn how to shuffle the cards, how to lay out a spread, and, finally, how to read what is in front of you.

CHAPTER THREE

The Court Cards and What They Mean

As you go through the meanings of the Tarot cards, you will see that some of the descriptions vary slightly. The subtle differences found in different Tarot decks will in no way affect their final meanings nor in any way influence the readings given them. Since Tarot is so widely used, variations from country to country are to be expected. As you choose your own deck, the best possible rule of thumb to use is: follow your own taste.

Every Tarot deck has the same number of cards, the same number of suits, and the same number of Court cards. The descriptions you are about to read may be applied to any deck you are likely to find for sale today.

You may decide to limit yourself to the least expensive deck you can find or you may decide to splurge on an elaborately decorated gypsy deck, but the results are the same, and the descriptions in this book are still applicable.

If you encounter two or more decks you like very

much and can't make up your mind which to buy, close your eyes for a moment and visualize each deck. Then take the one that pops into your mind first.

Now that you have chosen your own pack from among the many selections of European and American Tarot decks, examine the colorful pictures on the cards.

You will promptly notice that each card is different, unlike any other in the deck. The first twenty-two cards, numbered from zero through twenty-one, are called the Court cards. Their special names are printed at the bottom of each card. Following the Court cards are the four suits—Cups, Wands, Swords, and Pentacles—each with its King, Queen, Page, Knight, Ten, Nine, Eight, Seven, Six, Five, Four, Three, Two, and Ace. The fourteen cards in each suit and the twenty-two Court cards give us a total of seventy-eight cards.

The Tarot cards look nothing like a regular bridge or pinochle deck; the picture on each card takes the entire area of the card. It cannot be read from two directions like the conventional decks. Thus, in most Tarot spreads, when we see instructions telling us to reverse a given card, we know we are to turn that card upside down. A reversed card has a different meaning. The reversed meaning of each card in the Tarot deck is given after its conventional meaning.

Using this chapter as a guide, and putting your common sense and intuition to work for you, you should be able to make meaningful readings from the Tarot cards. The first twenty-two cards have deep spiritual significance. So that their meanings may be as clear to you as possible, I have taken pains to explain what these cards mean in relation to our nature and the parts of our existence to which they pertain.

As we begin with our explanations, note that the first three Court cards represent forces inside of us. The remaining nineteen cards deal with the end results of those forces.

Shall we begin?

THE FOOL—This card pictures a man dressed in the costume of a clown or jester. He carries a pack or stick over his shoulder. As a card, it is representative of the spirit within every man. Here is that part of each person which drives him from within as he journeys along the path of life. This spirit can cause man to be independent, to walk alone, and to be a complete person within himself, lacking all fear, guided by the knowledge that he himself has gleaned from living with nature. The Fool represents the individual who may be intuitive, the spirit of the artistic personality. In gypsy lore, it is said that the Fool "possesses the foolishness of God which is greater than the wisdom of men." Whether or not this spirit of adventure and originality makes for a better person depends on the individual's ability to put his awareness to intelligent use. Only on the rarest occasions can such perfection of mind and spirit be achieved.

The presence of the Fool in the spread does not represent an accomplished way of living but brings to light the tremendous spiritual forces with which the person in question is surrounded. It displays his desire to adapt himself to a way of life in keeping with his highest and most noble instincts. In general, the Fool represents the beginning of all creativity, and signifies the will to accomplish a desired goal, the highest point a man can set out to reach. A person with the Fool's nature rebels against all the established patterns of society, and lives life the way *he* sees fit. He is content with his own wisdom and seeks the adventures of life, not taking time to join any group or become part of any man-made project. He is on his own and, although he may run into society's rules and regulations, over he climbs, untouched by the obstacles, his eyes glowing with what he sees in the beautiful future.

In Reverse—If the Fool falls reversed, we may imply that the person makes faulty or foolish choices. Fear will hold him back from taking a chance. Life will make a fool of him. The joy and possibilities of adventure will never be attained. Unhappy conformity to the rules imposed by others characterizes his life.

THE MAGICIAN (Juggler, Wizard)—This card shows a man standing at a table upon which four suits of the Tarot are represented in the form of objects. One hand reaches up to take from what is above and the other hand rests upon the table or holds a wand. The

Magician represents the creation of new things, the beginning of new projects, the building of houses with foundations that will endure, and the great power of creativity. A person with the Magician's nature accepts the chances offered by life, takes the first step to success. He has thoughts about taking positive action which then take form and become tangible. This card signifies constructive power. A female's "magical powers" may lie in her ability to create a home. This woman may encourage and develop the character, personality, and skills of the young. She is an excellent teacher. In the male, this card may mean the presence of organizational skills which will soon be used to advantage in the reorganization of a department, the building of a company or even in the discovery of new scientific advances for the betterment of civilization. He who takes the opportunities offered by the Magician will find his life changed. These opportunities usually bring financial benefits.

In Reverse—Failure of projects, bad luck, a weak nature, a person whose love of himself makes him incapable of seeing anyone else clearly. The sacrifice of love and warmth for the attainment of success, which leads to ultimate unhappiness though money and fame are attained.

THE HIGH PRIESTESS—Here is a woman seated upon a throne placed between two pillars, one dark and one light, representing the obvious and the secret. She is beautifully robed and wears a crown upon her head. She holds a scroll half hidden beneath her robes. A moon is at her feet. She is the spirit of woman, the essence of all that is female. She is the woman every man sees when he is in love. She represents the mature basic intelligence we all have. She is the end result of learning now applied to the creation of new things. She is that wisdom of life which is possessed by woman, giving her the ability to guide children and to give strength to a man. She is all the beauty of nature personified. She is the silent part of all women that tells them how to behave with all people and especially men. She is female intuition and also that gentle force behind the success of great men. In her silent manner she is with the man she loves at all times, giving him strength with her love. She is the perfect woman all men dream of meeting. She exists in *all* women once they have discovered what their true role in a man's life must be. She gives all and takes nothing. It is from her that all Of Life originally comes. She is the "mother of invention." She is the spirit of woman, the spirit of motherhood. She is associated with the earth from which all things grow.

A man finding this card in his spread has this kind of love and this type of wise woman in his life. She will guide him to happiness and success and give him all the strength to cope with life's problems. A woman finding the High Priestess in her spread will realize these qualities within herself and using them wisely will feel that she has reached the ultimate purpose of her mission on earth. If this card represents a female friend she will be a comfort and a joy to know, always kind and full of understanding.

In Reverse—This card now tells of the presence of a selfish and ruthless woman who may destroy a man with her hunger for all that he can offer her. She will take all and leave behind the ruined shell of a human being. If a female is questioning the cards, the High Priestess may represent a life of drinking, cheating, extramarital relationships, overeating, taking drugs, and, in general, self-destruction.

THE EMPRESS—Here we see a woman seated upon a throne in a field of flowers or corn. She is wearing a flowered gown and her hair is loose about her shoulders. In her right hand she holds a scepter. The first three cards have dealt with the spirit. This is the first card of the manifest world or that which we can see and touch. The Empress represents fertility and means good luck for those who wish many children. This is a card of good crops, the reward of toil and mental labors is assured in a good harvest, and the successful accomplishment of studies. The Empress denotes action taken in all matters mixed with balance and stability: The full-face picture means openess of character and fair dealings in trade. This card predicts material wealth and a sound understanding of other people and their problems. The Empress is a "mother card." The everyday tasks of life will give an insight into the spirit. This is a card of contentment with everyday matters and a fruitful end to any project in question.

In Reverse—Fear and anxiety may lead to insanity. Poverty and famine will cause a broken home. The gypsy gives this reversal as an indication of war and plague.

THE EMPEROR—A regal man is shown seated upon a throne. He has a crown upon his head and holds a scepter and a glowing ball in his hands. He wears purple and ermine robes. The sun shines above his head. He has been likened to King Arthur, representing wisdom and the triumph of man over persecution and over suffering at the hands of others. This card predicts the domination of the intelligence over animal passions and greed for the material things. The Emperor is the card of self-mastery. It denotes stability, power, protection, authority, reasonable attitudes held by superiors, and it predicts the realization of great plans.

In Reverse—A weak character. Immaturity. Those still tied to their parents in adulthood; fear of authority; loss of self-control; possible loss of an inheritance to a thief; death in war, critical injury or the misrepresentation of facts with intent to defraud.

THE HIEROPHANT (The Pope, The High Priest)—A pope is seated upon a throne. One hand is raised in a blessing. Two men, cardinals or members of a congregation, kneel before him. This is the card for those of a spiritual or religious nature. It tells the ability of man to humble himself before God and, in so doing, to gain inner peace and strength. The possibility of a marriage or an alliance is suggested. Another account denotes inspiration, mercy, and servitude to mankind. It is also the card of religious leaders and doctors of the mind and body who have devoted their lives to the service of others.

In Reverse—Superstitious fears, doubt, renunciation of God and the Church; those who live contrary to the Ten Commandments, divorce.

THE LOVERS (Marriage, Eros)—Two naked figures, one male and one female, stand beneath a huge sun. The figure of an angel or cupid is shown within the sunburst. This is the card of predicaments and, if placed in the spread near a success card, predicts fulfillment of dreams and desires. The Lovers also represents man's desire for the pleasures of the spirit; there is a prediction of a battle between loyalty to one's mate and the desire to be unfaithful. Gypsies give this card the further meanings of love, attraction, beauty of body and soul. Here is the beginning of a romance and the desire to keep love virginal. The message of the Lovers is that "you cannot have your cake and eat it."

In Reverse—In-laws will interfere with a marriage. Marriage will become a trap, leading to infidelity, divorce, lawsuits. Children will be emotionally hurt by a broken home. Quarrels and a loss of love. A feeling of inadequacy in meeting day-to-day responsibilities.

THE CHARIOT—A prince is pictured in a chariot. He carries a sword. The Chariot is being drawn by two sphinxes, one black and one white. Material success is promised along with accomplishment in spiritual and artistic ventures. Triumph over enemies, sickness, and money difficulties. If the person questioning the cards is separated or divorced, a reconciliation is indicated. It is a card of a balanced life, mixing work with periods of travel and parties with times of productive solitude. Victory will come through hard work. Safety from accidents and recovery from grave illness is insured.

In Reverse—Defeat. Sudden collapse on the brink of success. Illness, general misfortune. Restlessness, superficial involvements. The "bar-fly" finding pleasure in empty conversation, seeking escape in love affairs with strangers. No interest in intellectual or spiritual pursuits. Gypsies say of this reversal, "Out of the strong comes forth sweetness, from the weak, the bitterness of misery." This card should be pondered by today's youth, who seek escape from responsibility and reality by taking drugs and who defeat their moral obligation to themselves by indulging in casual sexual relationships that lead to misery and lack of respect for both parties.

34

JUSTICE (The Scales)—A young woman is seated upon a throne with scales in her left hand and a sword in her right. In some Tarot decks, she is blindfolded. For the purpose of divination, this card represents balance, peace, and self-satisfaction in accomplishments. Another interpretation gives this card the balancing quality of Karma, the price that one must pay, after entering into the next life, for deeds committed in this lifetime. Justice represents the law of cause and effect based on the idea that "as one sows, so one shall reap." There is no possibility of getting away with something. The laws of natural justice prevail and man will always have to pay for what he has done.

In Reverse—In this position the card predicts injustice, false accusations, inequality, lawlessness, rioting, and violence as in the Watts and New York City riots. If this card falls reversed near the card of the Hanged Man, mercy and forgiveness will follow persecution.

THE HERMIT—An old and bearded man, dressed in monk's robes, wanders through the snow or the mountains carrying a lighted lantern. Here is the seeker of wisdom and truth. The Hermit is the wise man searching for the answer to all the unhappiness life can bring to people. The card predicts a meeting with one who will inspire the Querent (the person who asks the questions of the cards). It also predicts the acquisition of knowledge and protection from another. The seeker will always be a person of a curious but humble nature.

In Reverse—Refusing to accept growth and the responsibilities of maturity. Ignorance, foolish acts, childishness. One who lives in the past and refuses to go ahead and learn new things or to experience new ideas and meet new people.

THE WHEEL OF FORTUNE (Chance, Fate)—A wheel is pictured with seven spokes. Four animal heads, their species varying with Tarots of different countries, are shown in each of the four corners of the card. The words Rota and Taro may be written on the wheel to which two monkeys or youths are tied. The Wheel of Fortune is the turning wheel of life. It is fate, the cycles that man constantly experiences. It is joy, sorrow, birth, death, luck, misfortune; all the blows of fate that must be endured and all the joys that will follow misery by virtue of natural law. Seasons, harvest and famine, gain and loss, all take a turn, symbolized by the wheel. Man, bound to fate, is taken around and around in a never-ending series of cycles. The card predicts growth. There will be success after many setbacks. History will repeat itself and tomorrow may be probed as a repetition of yesterday. The constant turning of the wheel is also the theory of evolution. For every turn of the wheel a little more growth is created, a somewhat stronger, wiser, better-developed person emerges. What is happening in the Querent's life at the present time will pass into something better. As a result of suffering, man realizes the value of joy and sees old things with new insight. The past will offer new clues to the present and the future. The Wheel of Fortune predicts prosperity after famine and success after failure.

In Reverse—Fate will be unkind. Hard luck at every turn. Life will be an uphill battle. There will be long periods of suffering and misery but, eventually, peace and happiness will come. Also, self-torture and self-pity resulting from an inability to understand life as a seasonal, constantly growing process.

STRENGTH (Force)—A maiden, dressed in flowing robes, a garland of flowers on her head, stands against a lion; she is closing the lion's jaws with her hands. The symbol of infinity, a sideways figure eight, is above her head. The card denotes faith in one's self, confidence, courage, and the support of a loving woman who brings happiness to man. The ability of woman to endure pain and suffering as part of her natural makeup is suggested by the symbol-picture. A man finding this card in his spread will have such a female in his life. His strength will endure through all obstacles. A woman finding this card in her spread is being told that she has a strength and ability to overcome suffering through patience and the application of her femininity to everyday problems.

This card gives strength that will overcome the negative aspect of any surrounding cards of disaster. The symbol of infinity indicates that woman represents creation, and this knowledge of her inner strength gives woman the ability to face any fearful situation and to calm the people involved, guiding them away from unhappiness in a gentle but firm manner.

In Reverse—The influence of a selfish woman will lead to emotional instability and financial destruction. Weakness of character and physical illness. Impotency. Violent temper causing others grief. Giving in to temptations leading to defeat in business and love. Disgrace.

THE HANGED MAN—A young boy is shown hanging upside down from a scaffold. Leaves sprout from the wood. He is suspended from one ankle; the other leg is crossed over. There is a halo or glow about his head. This is the card of a man at the crossroads of life. It denotes a person of indecision, a dreamer who cannot accept everyday responsibilities because they interfere with his sense of idealism. It is also the card of the artist or the nonconformist; his actions are contrary to established conventions and place him in an inverted position to the dictates of society. He will suffer and martyr himself for his beliefs. This is also the card of the religious fanatic who, like the Buddhist monks today, will burn themselves to death to prove a point. This card represents idealism, possible martyrdom, talent, youth in need of guidance and understanding. While it may indicate the sacrifice of life, it is also the card of spiritual growth.

In Reverse—A crime committed and never discovered, hardships overcome. Legal victory; suicide prevented; a device long forgotten, then rediscovered.

DEATH—A skeleton dressed in black robes riding a horse. He carries a bloody scythe. Though the card may predict actual death it is an ancient gypsy tradition that this never be revealed to the Querent by the Reader. The suggestion of death may cause such great fear as to trigger tragedy that could have been avoided. It is always best to read this card in the light of its other possible meanings: rebirth, the conclusion of a part of one's life making way for new experiences, hope; complete despair will give way to hope and new promise of a better life. The gypsy does not give Death the meaning of finality; rather, "man dies many times before his death." The Death card predicts great change in a person's life. The nature of the change is clarified by the other cards surrounding this picture-symbol. If the card falls next to a Court card not representing the Querent, the change will occur through that person and affect the Querent as a result of his relationship with that other person.

In Reverse—Birth. Restoration of a broken home.

Order will follow chaos. New enterprise will present itself shortly.

TEMPERANCE—The picture is of a winged angel, with a star upon her forehead. She pours water from one pitcher into another. The meaning here is change, reconciliation or remarriage, self-control, and discipline. All projects will be completed in time. A ship will make a successful crossing. Life will be balanced with all areas of physical and mental pursuit bearing fruit.

In Reverse—Drunkenness, hostility, fighting and separation, a disaster at sea or death by drowning, sterility, all desire unfulfilled. Drug addiction, prostitution; crimes will be committed.

THE DEVIL (Satan, Lucifer)—A tall, well-built, naked male figure with batwings, taloned hands, and hooved feet sits upon a throne. He has a tail and his flesh is scaled. A man and a woman are chained to the altar upon which he is enthroned. They are all surrounded by flames. The card predicts that money dishonestly gained will be lost. Power achieved through cruelty to others will crumble. The perverse sexual life and disregard for human dignity are the personality traits of this card. It is the card of the Marquis de Sade. It is also the misery of the materialist who has lost his soul in his hunger and relentless drive to gain power over others.

In Reverse—A petty, spiteful person, lack of creative drive, lazy, no will to succeed or to improve himself. Money troubles, inability to reach a decision. Weak and timid, afraid of own shadow. These people, though useless to themselves and society, are not necessarily bad people and are often sentimental in their attitudes toward life.

THE TOWER (The House of God)—This card shows a tower, similar to the tower of a castle, being shattered by lightning, with hail and brimstone falling around it. Two men, either clothed or naked, fall from the tower. The meaning of the card is catastrophe. The causes of this calamity are the acts of God—the devastating results of natural forces such as tornadoes, twisters, tidal waves, and the like. There will be distress and misery, poverty, fighting within the home and the community, theft by neighbors and friends. The card may also denote a change of home and the loss of faith in one's self or in mankind. These disasters will pass and within one season all will adjust and happiness will return.

In Reverse—False accusations. Domination by a tyrant. Freedom of spirit and body will be gained at great cost. This card in reverse position foretold the reign of such men as Hitler. Going back in history, it anticipated the crucifixion of Jesus Christ and the terror of the Inquisition. In general, this reverse position means that

41

eventually the good in man will win out over the restraint of unjust and selfish leaders. This can easily apply to a family situation rather than a nation.

THE STAR—A naked woman kneels with her left knee on the earth and her right foot in the flowing water. She holds two pitchers from which she pours water upon the earth and back into the flowing water. This is the card of inspiration. There will be contact with one who will give this inspiration. There will be new perception of mental and spiritual things. Intuition will be heightened. Good health will follow a period of illness. Strength and potency will climb to new heights. The Star has been called the card of destiny. The Querent will meet with a person who will give new hope and strength to his life. For a woman, this card in her spread means a man will come into her life who will be the most important person she has ever met. He will be her great love and give her a new "lease on life." This person, represented by the card of destiny, whether male or female, will shape the destiny of the Querent and remain in his or her life in some fashion until the Querent's death.

In Reverse—Bad luck or disaster. Lack of perception. Materialism and dull-headedness. Physical and mental illness.

THE MOON—A full moon is shown in a sky full of stars. A wolf and a dog bay at the silver light. A lake or small body of water is shown at the foot of the card from which a crayfish or serpent rises. If a crayfish, its claws are upraised toward the moon. This card predicts unforeseen perils to those one loves. Security in general is in danger. Badly placed in the spread it tells of insanity which may follow great mental instability. If well placed, such as the central card, it denotes peace, visions come to reality, calmness of mind, and the victory of the soul over the terrors of the mind. Fear will be driven back to the place from which it had no right to come.

In Reverse—Imagination crushed by conventionality, recovery from a nervous breakdown, peace of mind but at great cost. Failure in examinations or on the path of the spirit. In any position the card denotes the power of the full moon to cloud reality, veil reason, and bring events to a climax. Only in the center of the spread can the card denote any logic or comprehension. If reversed in the center all will work out well but at the cost of a period of great fear and instability. This is a bad card for lovers. Love will win out but not before it is almost destroyed by fear, envy, and many misunderstandings.

THE SUN—A huge, brilliant sun is shown above a naked child riding a white horse. The child carries a banner. The significance is assured success, gay reunions, good health, release from any type of imprisonment, completion of all projects, pleasure in the simple life, and the acceptance of a great and triumphant future.

In Reverse—The future becomes cloudy. Failure is met at every turn, a loved one lost, a difficult childbirth, broken engagement, loss of a valued object.

JUDGMENT—The angel of the day of judgment appears in the clouds blowing his trumpet. Below, the tombs of the dead open and those within rise up naked, their hands clasped in prayer. This card predicts the satisfactory accomplishment of work well done, regeneration of mind or body after a period of suffering and waste, triumph over all odds, a legal judgment in one's favor. Friendship exalted. The renunciation of the married state.

In Reverse—Loss of goods. Failure to find happiness in old age. Divorce or separation. Disillusionment. Diseases of the eyes, ears, or heart.

THE WORLD—A nude woman, her only covering a flowing veil. She is encircled in a wreath of laurel roses and lilies. The symbols of the four elements—earth, air, fire, and water—are placed in each of the four corners of the card. This is the last card of the twenty-two Trump cards of higher arcana, as it is called in most texts. The world represents completion of all things and success and triumph, the fulfillment of all desires, high and low. Reason will ascend over emotion giving strength and great understanding of life's meaning. There will be travel, change of home, change in the means of livelihood. Man is no longer bound to unnecessary circumstances because he lacks awareness of his own abilities. Man is now free to move ahead with his new-found knowledge and succeed in all undertakings. With his great understanding of life and other people, he has the ability to make others happy and to give wisely. Anyone having this card in their spread will find this ultimate happiness, is capable of it, and needs only to realize the meanings of the other twenty-one cards and this high state of being will bring peace and joy to the Querent and those around him.

In Reverse—Stubbornness, attachment to one place or profession, lack of vision.

Now that we've seen the Court cards, let's move on to the four suits: Cups, Wands, Swords, and Pentacles.

CHAPTER FOUR

The Suit of Cups

Within the Cups we will find all our passions from the most base to the highest. Cups promise pleasure, gaiety, laughter, and joy. Cups can promise permanence, stability, good health, and freedom from the cares of the world. However, the Cups may also warn of laziness, self-indulgence, and indifference to the welfare of others. Cups usually offer the Querent, the person questioning the cards, a choice between the calm inner joys of contemplation and unselfish giving to others or the more involved pleasures of sacrifice for material gain.

This suit deals with fair people who have blond hair and light complexions. These people are not always honest, but have good, warm hearts; they are often saddened or of a melancholy temperament. They often make law their profession and can be born into a family of "old money." They are usually kind and love people, and are often deeply religious. They follow one of two distinct paths in marriage. Either they are true and loyal forever or they are constantly involved in cheating on their mate and, in general, making married life miserable because of their own selfish indulgence in sex, gambling, drinking, and joining single people in wild night life. These people are so emotional that they may literally "die for love."

THE KING—He holds a scepter and a cup, his throne is upon a sea, containing a fish and perhaps a boat. He is fair complexioned. When the King falls in the Querent's spread, he is skilled in law or is a merchant. He is a member of the church and supports it in all ways. He is balance, peace, art and science explored, good thinking, and originality. Kind and considerate of others, he takes responsibility and does not shirk his duties.

In Reverse—Dishonest, two-faced, a liar. He loves scandal and is a trickster. Vicious and self-centered, he is a seducer who can hurt many women by his endless taking. He gives nothing in return. Beware of being parted from your money or love by this man.

THE QUEEN—A fair and beautiful woman, one who has rich intuitive powers on which she can rely. She is romantic and a dreamer, but she can be down to earth and practical. Good with money, she is honest and devoted to her family and friends. She encourages everyone, gaining pleasure from their success. She represents the perfect wife and mother.

In Reverse—A brilliant but unreliable woman. Skilled in the art of selling herself, she can use people until they have no more to give her. Then she will turn on them or disappear from their lives. She loves no one but herself. She can lead a man to financial ruin and destroy an entire family.

THE KNIGHT—A young, graceful man upon a horse, carrying a cup in one hand. He is clearly younger than the King. He signifies the beginning of new projects. He brings business proposals, social invitations, and is the bearer of important messages.

In Reverse—An artificial man, sly, and cunning. He suggests fraud. He lies easily and has little depth. He can cause trouble for a husband as a seducer of wives.

THE PAGE—A blond boy, younger than the Knight, holding a cup out of which rises a fish. A young man in his early twenties, he represents the formation of the creative mind. He is a lover of the arts and a deep thinker. He gives good advice to his friends and associates on all matters and is loyal to his fraternities and his close friends. He will offer his services freely and help out in troubled situations without being asked. He would change a tire for you as soon as needed. He would ask nothing in return.

In Reverse—A rebellious youth. Good taste but no desire to create. He is a seducer and a flirt, hurting those who love him. He is attached to his friends and shirks his responsibilities to his family. He may drink and smoke at an early age and take drugs for "kicks." He was the same as a teen-ager and has little hope of changing in the future although now he is in his early twenties.

TEN—A rainbow is shown over a family group with children. This card signifies love, peace, harmony, and friendship, and is also representative of one's own home town or property. It denotes successful agreements, partnerships, and fruitful contracts.

In Reverse—Rage, criminal actions, circumstances forcing one to take drastic measures. Guilt feelings will come.

NINE—The card pictures one who is surrounded by cups filled with joy and material possessions. It means goodwill to others, happiness and satisfaction with what one has accomplished and attained. Advantageous meetings. Success and victory. Material and spiritual wealth.

In Reverse—False freedom, too great a sense of material possessions. A misplaced truth, a sentimental nature leading to weakness and failure. A tendency to think that the bad traits in another will vanish. Danger of a robbery while possessions are unguarded.

EIGHT—A dejected-looking man is pictured. He is offered a cup but turns away from it. Shyness is indicated here, also meekness, modesty, and enjoyment of quiet pleasure. A studious person.

49

In Reverse—Disillusion with possessions or money troubles. There is a possibility of happiness through jolly company.

SEVEN—Many cups are shown holding varied treasures. Some contain serpents and women with snakes instead of hair. One cup is covered. It is surrounded by a glow. The card indicates vivid imagination. The Querent is clairvoyant. Experiences of the past have not given inner peace. The future holds a deep and beautiful experience, just for the taking. There is a hunger for that which is beautiful. A strong will.

In Reverse—Plans that are just dreams will not come to pass. Foolishness and daydreaming lead to failure in business and love.

SIX—Children in a garden, gathering flowers. They exchange flowers which are put into baskets. This is the card of the past. It denotes tender recollections and nostalgia. There is a desire to change everything and make all new. Originality will bring dreams to reality. This card may represent old love letters or pressed flowers that hold fond memories for the Querent.

In Reverse—Plans will fail. While the Querent dreams of bringing back the past, another has taken his or her place with the beloved.

FIVE—A man stands before a bridge. A castle is on the far side of a river. Three cups are overturned. Two remain standing. This card denotes love until death. An inheritance will come. One may be asked to offer one's life for another. A marriage of arrangement may be in the offing.

In Reverse—Despair. Faith in blood lines rather than talents. A weak person. Another meaning is death of a loved one or parting forever. The gypsies attribute the tragedy of Romeo and Juliet to this card in a reversed position.

FOUR—A youth seated below a tree is offered a cup from a hand reaching out of a cloud. The card denotes unhappiness and bitter experiences, a desire to find happiness and change established patterns, a disgust with physical passions and a desire for spiritual happiness.

In Reverse—Excesses of all kinds. Fatigue, bad health. Rejected by a loved one.

THREE—Three maidens dance in a field of newly harvested vegetables or flowers. The meaning here is that all will end well. Harvest, comfort, speedy success are key symbols.

In Reverse—Famine. Illness, delays, loss of prestige. Sexual passions without love.

TWO—A man and a woman exchange cups beneath the mythical sign of Hermes. This card means love, a deep friendship, spiritual and physical union.

In Reverse—Divorce, separation, a husband or wife

will be unfaithful. A friend will turn against the Querent. Vows will be broken. The end of a love affair with both parties remaining friends but never again lovers. Jealousy and vindictive action. The desire for revenge.

ACE—An angel holds a cup from which pours water, flowers, or doves. This card is the ultimate of love. It represents fertility of mind, body, and spirit. It predicts a glorious marriage and many children. It can mean a bountiful harvest. It is the happiest and most fruitful card in the suit of Cups.

In Reverse—Divorce, hate, sterility, a love that cannot be because one or the other party is unwilling and will never change. Unrequited love, famine, floods, loss of money will result.

CHAPTER FIVE

The Suit of Wands

The Wands concern people who are fair and honest in character but often dark in complexion. Wands are cards of enterprise, sociability, and usefulness. Though the Wands people are usually social and do well in business enterprises, they are quite modest, humble, and they give in to the arrows of fate rather than fight. The suit deals with spiritual or earthly gain and all the problems related to these desires. These are the cards of merchants and day-to-day activities of trade and its effect on personality and the home life.

KING—A handsome man with a well-built agile body is seated upon a throne. He holds a flowering wand. Lions decorate the back of his throne. He represents a man of high ancestry. He is loyal, honest, a devoted friend. He is usually married. He generally will live in the country or suburbs of a city. In all activities he is well balanced and understanding of the needs of others.

In Reverse—High principles and an exaggerated idea of right and wrong. Severe and often ruthless. Foolishly tolerant of people that will do him more harm than good. The gypsies liken him to Julius Caesar.

QUEEN—An exquisite woman, exotic in bone structure, sensual and magnetic, is seated upon a throne holding a wand in flower. A black cat is at her feet. When the Queen of Wands falls in a Querent's spread, she is intelligent and fertile. She is honest and loves her home and loves the outdoor world of nature. She is practical with money and has good business sense. She is so beautiful that men constantly chase after her but she is faithful to her husband and would never consider leaving her family or her mate for a meaningless escapade. She is devoted to domesticity, and is delicate and full of feminine grace and charm.

In Reverse—A woman who is thrifty to the point of being penny pinching. She is deeply jealous, unstable in her emotions, and cannot be trusted. She will lie easily and, at the slightest hint of coldness from her husband, will take a lover.

KNIGHT—A Knight in armor rides his horse in a hasty motion. He carries a wand. He represents a man younger than the King and he lives by intuition rather than judgment. He is always in a hurry. He is very attractive to women. He indicates change, journey over water and land, or sudden flight from one place to another.

In Reverse—Quarreling, breaking up of a marriage or an engagement, work interfered with because of emotional problems, or the refusal to give another his or her freedom.

PAGE—A young boy, younger than the Knight, is pictured standing with his wand. He represents a lover that may enter a woman's life, or he may represent a telegraph boy or a messenger who will bring an unusual piece of news. He is capable of breaking women's hearts because he feels nothing for them. He is generally lazy; although he comes from wealth, he himself is poor.

In Reverse—One who is unable to make decisions and is generally unable to cope with day-to-day problems. A gossip.

TEN—A man carrying ten wands, which weigh heavily upon him. This card denotes the problems of too much success, or the guilt of presenting a false appearance for gain. He is one who is heavy with worry and fear.

In Reverse—A traitor, a liar, one who will cause great difficulties in other's lives.

NINE—A man resting upon his wand in the middle of a road. The card means hidden enemies are near. The need to face up to conflict and the strength to overcome trouble is within the Querent. Bravery in self-defense.

In Reverse—Delay, worry, disaster, and bad luck will have to be challenged.

EIGHT—Eight wands are shown across the card. Motion and change are indicated. A journey will come that will lead to a new way of life. There will be swift action, decisions made in a hurry.

In Reverse—The Querent will be quick to reach out for happiness and love without giving necessary thought to his action. Jealousy, hasty messages, fights, a guilty conscience. There is a danger here of being forced to spend much time alone.

SEVEN—A man stands on the edge of a cliff holding his wand in a gesture of defense in combat. The card predicts many foes in business. It is indicative of an executive position challenged. Here is the suggestion of arguments, wise money transactions. Success in trials and examinations.

In Reverse—Hesitancy will cause great loss. A baffling question will confuse the Querent. No answer will come because he fears taking action in any direction.

SIX—A horseman carries a wand wreathed with laurel and roses. Other persons follow behind, awed by his glory. The card means victory, success, and good news for all involved. Waiting will be resolved into fulfilled desires.

In Reverse—Vague fears cloud optimism. Delay in affairs. The feeling that enemies are about to attack. Jealousy may lead to battle between rival companies.

FIVE—A group of young men, each with a wand, crowd together, beating each other with staffs. The card denotes that the games people play in this life in order to succeed will lead to misery. This is the card of tests constantly being thrown in our paths, also unquenchable thirst for money and power. The card predicts that greed will lead to misery and perhaps total failure. There will be success but it will not be appreciated and will not satisfy. This is the card of the gambler who won't quit while he's ahead and who will eventually lose everything he has won.

In Reverse—A lawsuit will come. A partner will try to cheat the company. Beware of trickery in business. Trust no one with accounts or vital secrets should this card fall reverse near a Court card.

FOUR—Two women carry baskets or garlands of flowers cross a stream or walk under a pavilion made of flowering wands. The Four prophesies material security with a house in the country and vast real-estate holdings. There is a promise of happiness bought by money.

This is the card of the "newly rich" who tend to overdo everything so that they may impress others.

In Reverse—Loss of everything. There is no real security in money when it replaces the security that comes from knowing one's own self. When material things replace the gifts of the spirit, the loss of material wealth will destroy everything and everyone who has made money the foundation of their life.

THREE—A merchant stands on a hill looking out to sea where his ships pass with his merchandise. He rests upon one wand, two other wands surround him. Practical help will come in time of trouble. A man with an honest and kind nature will give of himself and end problems.

In Reverse—The loss of goods at sea. A sense of being cast adrift from society. Rejection by friends. One will try to trick you by giving unsound advice in time of great trouble.

TWO—A man dressed in princely garments watches the world from the tower of his castle. He holds a globe symbolizing the world in one hand. In the other he holds a wand. Riches and power will be offered in place of love and marriage. A woman will be asked to become a mistress to a wealthy man. A wealthy but unhappy man will come into the Querent's life.

In Reverse—Loss of faith in mankind. A childless

marriage. A marriage for money. Love will die. The spirit will be denied, causing unhappiness even though there will be money and power.

ACE—The hand of God holds a flowering wand, descending from a cloud. This card denotes fertility, creativity on all planes and presages a family rich with love, children, riches, and great happiness. The children will carry on the family business.

In Reverse—Decadence, pride that leads to ruin. Vast wealth but the destruction of happiness through greed. The card predicts the most miserable kind of emptiness, the emptiness of the spirit. Great wealth will be useless, love cannot be bought, happiness cannot be found through materialism. An empty but materially successful existence.

CHAPTER SIX

The Suit of Swords

The Swords are the cards of war, high ideals, and heroic battles. They are the representation of the cold, methodical, but equitable people. In the suit of Swords one finds the deepest misery that can be endured, the deepest fears, and the greatest joys of conquest of personal problems. The people of the suit of Swords can be either light or dark complexioned, but in their personal appearance they appear "gray." They show little emotion on the surface. They are dedicated to particular causes and when they love, their high ideals and militant attitude toward life make them intense but romantic. These people take life seriously to such a degree that they often destroy themselves with their violent intensity. They have a deep and at times impossible desire to make justice prevail.

The Sword people have little gaiety in their lives. If not actually soldiers, they are dedicated executives, brilliant mathematicians, or doctors. These people are more mental than physical in their personal relations and, if they marry, they must mate with their own kind. The sensitive nature of the Swords is buried and only a person who is thoroughly understanding of this type of personality can live happily with a Sword type. They are prone to terrible tempers and rages and when they show the other side of their dualistic nature they are almost childlike in their wonderment at the sacred and holy part that love plays in their emotions. Though they may encounter many different relationships during a lifetime, the Sword type, once pledging his love to one person, will never stop loving the object of his affections. The insane geniuses of history were usually among this group of Sword people.

KING—A man with a stern face and posture sits upon a throne, holding his sword. He represents power and strength, authority, law and order. He is brilliant and takes part in all matters pertaining to the running of a business or country. He has the wisdom of Solomon and, though unbending in his decisions, may still be merciful.

In Reverse—A sadist. One who would plan the overthrow of a home or of his own country. Because of his brilliant mind he is very dangerous.

QUEEN—A woman, regal but cold in manner, sits upon a throne, holding a sword and resting its hilt upon the arm of her seat. Her hand is held out in a gesture of generosity. She is one who has suffered greatly. She is strict with those around her but still kind. She represents one who has suffered a great loss. She may be sterile or in mourning for a loved one whom she will never be able to replace. She is wise beyond her years. No one can fathom her, but all respect her. Everything she does is done to perfection.

In Reverse—One who is prudish and given to gossiping. She is vengeful and will go to any lengths to get even. Her brilliant mind, like that of the King, makes her a treacherous enemy.

KNIGHT—A man nearing middle age, astride his horse, advances at a gallop. His sword is raised. This type of person is good at heart, courageous, and an excellent soldier of high rank. He shows these traits in his business activities. His offices are run like a military camp. He is dramatic in his mannerisms, powerful and strong in all things. He is not afraid of life and will challenge unhappiness and usually win over any obstacles. He is cold and efficient but feels deeply, although he does not show his sentiments openly. He is dedicated to those he loves but is not open in his romanticism. When he shows love, it is deep and meaningful. He is shrewd and cannot be deceived.

In Reverse—Quick in everything he does, he is constantly in trouble. He spends too much money to impress others and acts on impulse rather than on sound judgment.

PAGE—A very young man, perhaps twenty or so, holds his sword with both hands as he walks over the countryside through clouds and rain. He is a bright boy, and because of his basic intelligence, which will grow into brilliance, he is well placed as a diplomat perhaps or as a vice-consul in an embassy, despite his youth. He is fair in his dealings but is somewhat introverted and is given to spying.

In Reverse—The card in this position predicts that the unforeseen will happen—illness or a weakened mental condition. The worst time will come when the moon is full; great depression will follow.

TEN—A man is shown face down on the ground; he is pierced by ten swords. The card indicates that suffering and misery, tears, mental anguish, and pain will come. Trouble will come despite money and high position. Someone will ask for charity.

In Reverse—Anguish will continue for a long time because of mental inability to overcome problems. Great loss. The sun will not shine in the life of a Ten-type person for a long period of time.

NINE—A woman is shown in deep sorrow. Her hands cover her face. The meaning here is that news comes to the Querent of the death of someone close. There will be sorrow over another. A loved one may be unfaithful. Another interpretation carries the meaning of shame and disgrace, a secret love affair uncovered, or disease of the reproductive organs.

In Reverse—A young girl will lose her virginity. Scandal and slanderous gossip will prevail. A broken marriage, caused by another woman or man.

EIGHT—A chained woman is shown walking away from a dark castle. Her chains are falling away. The card denotes imprisonment for a period of time, being forced into patterns of life which are not the Querent's choice, domination by a cruel person. This will pass in time and freedom will be regained.

In Reverse—Bad news, terror of the unknown, hard work, a depressed state of mind.

SEVEN—A group of men are pictured, setting up a camp. There are tents and banners in the background. The card denotes a wish about to be fulfilled, new plans, self-assurance, good luck.

In Reverse—Quarrels over plans that have failed. A lot of arguments over petty little problems.

SIX—A man, a woman, and a child are shown in a rowboat, heading toward a distant island. The indication is that there will be a journey by water. There will be an offer of marriage. The future will be easy to cope with.

In Reverse—Sudden publicity is imminent. Look for an unwanted proposal, either financial or romantic.

FIVE—A victorious knight is pictured, holding the swords of his enemies. The conquered adversaries are shown walking away in dejection. The card foretells conquest. There is a warning here to be considerate of those less fortunate or they may turn against the Querent out of jealousy.

In Reverse—There will be a funeral of an associate where the Querent will encounter people he has known for a long while.

FOUR—A man is shown in a position of prayer. A lighted window shines above him. The card denotes temporary seclusion. The card indicates peace and tranquility although the Querent is alone.

In Reverse—There will be a desire to bring back what is lost. The Querent feels hopeless and will make a will in advance of death. (This is not a prophecy of death, but denotes a person in a depressed state of mind.)

THREE—A heart is pictured pierced with three daggers. The card denotes that strife will give strength.

There will be a delay in projects, there will be upheaval in the home or business.

In Reverse—Separation, mental incompatibility, political strife.

TWO—A young girl, blindfolded, is seated on a stone. She holds two crossed swords. The indication here is friendship with people in the military, tender relations giving strength to others. Balance and harmony.

In Reverse—There is a feeling of impending danger. Danger of masochism. Imposters will try to trick the Querent.

ACE—A hand is shown emerging from a cloud. A sword is held in the hand. The Ace of Swords is a card of success. The ability to love or hate another will come to the force. A child will be born who will become famous. Strong emotions will be brought out by a business or romantic involvement.

In Reverse—Self-destruction. Violent tempers will cause trouble. The best and worst of a person's personality will be brought out. There will be a great loss in business or romance.

CHAPTER SEVEN

The Suit of Pentacles

A pentacle is a five-pointed star. The suit of Pentacles relates to the dark and psychic people. The Pentacles relate to agriculture, the arts, and the sciences. There is no other suit so deeply emotional or so prone to the "up and down" periods that we all experience. The men and women of this suit are philosophical. They are easily hurt because of a deep sensitivity, but are wise enough to understand others and to forget. The artists, poets, and authors come from this suit as do many theatrical people. On the other hand, because these people so well understand the cycles and very intricate balance of nature, the most successful farmers, builders, and agricultural scientists are included in this suit. The Pentacles people are prone to visions, prophetic dreams, and all types of psychic experiences. They make wonderful partners in marriage but are not suited to the regimentation and coldness of "raw business." They are happier and more productive in the country than in the city. They are "children of nature." The men of this suit are in love with life and are as warm and outgoing as the women. A negative type may never be able to settle down to practical living. Generally, they are so involved with the aesthetic side of life and the world of the spirit that the thought of just working in a day-to-day kind of environment literally makes them sick! If all the wisdom, coming naturally to this sign, is directed and disciplined we have as an end result the great artists, writers, scientists, and inventors.

KING—A dark man is seated upon a throne. He holds a pentacle. He is brave, intelligent, virile, excellent as a mathematician, and a loyal friend. As a husband he is unsurpassed, as a lover the most affectionate mate possible. He sees the good in a person before the bad and will give all he has for a loved one. He is firm in his ideas and tends to see events in terms of black and white. His philosophies are dear to him; though unselfish in his attitudes, he will rebel if pushed too far. If after many chances a person still intrudes on his conceptions he will close them out of his life to such a degree that he considers the person nonexistent. Because he may tend to live in a dream world he may hurt a person without realizing it. When the incident is called to his attention, he will make amends with grand gestures of affection or expensive gifts.

In Reverse—A man easy to bribe, extravagant to a

fault, one who can be easily tempted to unfaithfulness, drunkenness, and excess of all kinds, including overeating and the use of drugs.

QUEEN—A dark woman is seated on her throne in a garden of flowers. She looks deeply into the pentacle which she holds in her hand. Rich but generous, she sees beneath the surface of all things and understands the truth of all that is presented to her. She is a defender of man's freedom and liberty, and, though she will fight for a cause she believes in, she will never lose her grace and dignity. She has many friends and is loyal to them. She is a devoted wife and worships her husband. She understands her own shortcomings and places no burden of responsibility upon her mate. She is psychic and can be a valuable ally or a vicious and frightening enemy.

In Reverse—A cruel and vicious person, full of suspicion and fear. She lives in a constant state of suspense and anxiety. She trusts no one, including herself.

KNIGHT—A dark young man is shown riding upon a horse. He holds a pentacle in his hand. The card denotes a man, in his early thirties, given to philosophical studies who usually makes his fortune as an educator in many fields. He lives well and surrounds himself with beauty and "the good things of life."

In Reverse—Narrow-mindedness, too much preoccupation with material gain. Limited by dogmatic views, he cannot understand another's position.

PAGE—A youth is pictured here holding a pentacle which appears to be floating in his hand. He stands in a garden or on a fertile hill. The card denotes a studious personality. One who is in his or her late teens or early twenties. The Page denotes the formation of ideas and philosophies; he is the "beautiful dreamer," one who will give advice freely though his ideas are not necessarily sound.

In Reverse—Rebelliousness. Nonconformity leading to adverse social criticism. In this position the card denotes today's beatnik or hippie.

TEN—A man, woman, and child are pictured with a dog and an old man. They walk toward a house. The card means the acquisition of possessions, an inheritance.

In Reverse—A problem concerning illegitimacy, danger of a burglary, bad news through the mail, loss through gambling.

NINE—A woman stands in a garden; she carries a tame bird. The card denotes safety in material possessions. Foresight, wisdom, the accumulation of wealth.

In Reverse—Storms, crops destroyed, danger of thieves.

EIGHT—A sculptor is pictured at work at his bench. The card predicts the beginning of new undertakings that will bring much success. There will be new orders for the businessman and old debts will be paid. The card also denotes one who is skillful with his hands.

In Reverse—Failure of ambitions, disillusionment, vanity, dishonest dealings in business.

SEVEN—A young man studies a bush from which pentacles grow like flowers. The card denotes successful dealings and many transactions involving large sums of money.

In Reverse—A loan will not be repaid; there is fear over lack of money; creditors will call and cause anxiety; impudent actions will cause trouble among associates.

SIX—A beautifully dressed merchant carries a pair of scales. He gives alms to beggars. Kindness of heart is indicated here. It will bring wealth and success in business. The Querent will be looked upon favorably by associates.

In Reverse—Loss of money. Thieves will break into a store. There will be slanderous gossip about the Querent. Evil deeds committed in the past will cause problems in the future.

FIVE—Three beggars walk in the snow, under a lighted window. The card means that people will be brought together through similar problems.

In Reverse—Lovers will not be able to marry. A job may be lost. A mistress will call upon her lover's wife and threaten the marriage. There will be guilt causing emotional problems. Marriage will fail through lack of understanding or sexual frigidity.

FOUR—Two men are shown in an embrace. The card denotes an inheritance. Events will come to pass happily after much delay.

In Reverse—Keep your possessions well guarded. Anxiety and obstacles will have to be overcome.

THREE—An artist is shown painting in a church. The card denotes money received for artistic work. The Querent is artistic, spiritual, and highly skilled in the arts or sciences.

In Reverse—Position is endangered by another's envy. Daydreams will stop creativity. Malicious gossip and money troubles.

TWO—A male dancer is pictured, holding two pentacles which he juggles within the symbol of infinity. The card denotes that happy social events will come. There will be much celebrating. A letter will arrive pointing to the end of many troubles.

In Reverse—Enforced gaiety, anxiety, fear of losing a job or a loved one. There is a danger of drunkenness leading to an accident.

ACE—A hand, emerging from a cloud, holds a pentacle. The card denotes success, happiness, the full understanding of the beauty of nature. The ability to endure trouble until the trouble turns into joy, is indicated. There will be money in the bank and material possessions.

In Reverse—Greed, fear over loss of material possessions, pettiness, jealousy.

CHAPTER EIGHT

Guide to Cards — How to Begin

Here is a simple reminder of what we have learned about the Court cards. It is an extra little guide to help refresh your memory about these more difficult Tarot cards.

THE FOOL—Man on the journey of life. *Reversed*—Folly, thoughtless action.

THE MAGICIAN—The beginning of all things. *Reversed*—Bad luck, a weak nature.

THE HIGH PRIESTESS—The feminine essence, inspiration, love. *Reversed*—An evil, corrupt female; ruin, degradation.

THE EMPRESS—Fertility, growth, action. *Reversed*—Destruction, famine.

THE EMPEROR—Intelligence, power. *Reversed*—Weakness, mental instability.

THE HIEROPHANT—The power of the Church, love of God. *Reversed*—Sin, guilt.

THE LOVERS—Choice, love, marriage. *Reversed*— The corruption of man through his physical desires.

THE CHARIOT—Success, triumph. *Reversed*— Failure, loss of prestige.

JUSTICE—Balance, good fortune. *Reversed*— Injustice, misery, bad Karma.

THE HERMIT—Inspiration, prudence. *Reversed*— Ignorance, waste, disregard for the important things of life.

THE WHEEL OF FORTUNE—History repeats itself, good luck. *Reversed*—Destiny will be cruel, many problems to face.

STRENGTH—Force through gentleness. The power of woman. *Reversed*—Weakness.

THE HANGED MAN—Attainment through suffering for one's beliefs. *Reversed*—Misery, self-sacrifice for the wrong goals.

DEATH—Rebirth, new situations. *Reversed*—Bad news, loss of position.

TEMPERANCE—The middle of the road is best, all things in moderation. *Reversed*—Overindulgence, the extreme will create a drain, excess in all things, loss.

THE DEVIL—Loss of that which is dishonestly gained. *Reversed*—Pettiness, money troubles.

THE TOWER—The destruction of old, worn-out patterns; new designs will come. *Reversed*—Domination by a tyrant.

THE STAR—Destiny, intuition, new perception. *Reversed*—Lack of perception.

THE MOON—Everything follows a cycle. The unforeseen. *Reversed*—Imagination will be crushed.

THE SUN—New life, happiness, success. *Reversed*—Failure, loss of a valued object.

THE JUDGMENT—The advancement of position and self, reunion. *Reversed*—Divorce, disillusionment.

THE WORLD—Success in all things. *Reversed*—Lack of vision.

The Tarot cards include all situations and leave no person untouched. Through them, we have met all the men and women, all the events that one can imagine in a lifetime.

Have you decided yet which of the cards represents you? By now, this should not be difficult. Take a good objective look at yourself, noting size, complexion, hair coloring, and so forth. Add to this picture your basic personality traits. Now return to the deck and see if you can find the card that most closely approximates you. Sometimes, as you do this, you may be reminded of a person who is close to you. Fine, that's good practice, too. But don't stop your searching through the deck until you can find the one card that closely represents you. For in some people, the definitions I've given will fit perfectly. Others may note a strong similarity between themselves and two or more cards. If that should happen, try the legal approach and weigh all the evidence carefully. Then, being perfectly honest with yourself, chose the one card that has a preponderance of your qualities.

Now that you have yourself established in the Tarot deck, try your hand at selecting others. The better you are at this, the more effective your readings will be for yourself and for others.

Take the girl next door for an experiment. She's the sort who always greets you with a smile. Her house is spotless and, as grandmother used to say, "you could eat from her floors." The perfect wife and mother, she is the ideal Queen of Cups type.

Suppose you know a girl who is always reading. Which of the Tarot cards would represent her? She's the one who writes those endless poems and is constantly consulting books to look up something. She's the one you heard on the call-in radio show, discussing current events. She's also the girl who invites all the writers and artists in town to her home for an open house. Your family calls her an intellectual, but they might also call her a "kook." In any event, she sees many variations in the world around her. She's a deep thinker and a lovely person. She is a perfect Queen of Pentacles type.

Consider your own husband. Perhaps he's the captain of the Little League team. He is always there when you need him, and often when you don't. He moderates all the important family discussions, never forgets birthdays, is wise and kind, and just plain wonderful. He's the King of Cups type.

Then there may be your brother to consider. Everyone who knows him adores him. But that's just about all he really offers anyone, his charm. How many times have you caught him sleeping when he should have been mowing the lawn, or off to the movies with his friends when there was weeding to be done or errands to be taken care of? He is our Page of Cups.

Suppose you are a working girl and you have a boss who never smiles. You've told your husband that, if Mr. Jones ever did smile, his face would crack! He counts every penny in petty cash and, if you are seven seconds late to work in the morning, he knows it. He even wears a stopwatch. His suits are always neat and pressed. His shoes are military shiny. When he cracks a joke you wonder what's so funny but smile politely. Mr. Jones is a very busy man, so tied up in charts and papers and telephones and important deals that, after it's all over for the day, you wonder if he ever loosens up and becomes a human being instead of a robot. Mr. Jones is the King of Swords. You'll get what you deserve from him, but you will definitely have to earn it.

Everyone has his own particular set of traits. If a

person's coloring doesn't exactly match his personality, according to the cards, remember that even in the wise Tarot there are exceptions to the rule. Let the basic qualities take preference over physical descriptions if you can't make an exact match.

Many years ago, I had the good fortune to travel in Spain, where I encountered the most fascinating person I have ever known. She was a true Spanish gypsy. After a bit of persuasion, she consented to read my cards. I was told that I would meet the dark King of Pentacles within a year and marry him. She pointed to the pentacle on the card and said that he would be a man of much money. That was the best news I'd heard for ages. I thanked the gypsy and waited to meet the dark, wealthy gentleman. A few months later, back in the United States, I walked into a local bank to deposit a birthday check. Hurrying through the door, I collided with a man who was holding a sack full of change. The sack hit the floor and spilled silver in every direction. The man, who was blond and fair, watched as I crawled around on the floor recovering the money; he thought the incident was very funny. We became friends and I learned that Bill was a writer and a student of religion and philosophy. After a courtship filled with lectures and visits to homes of professors and other writers, Bill and I were married. The King of Pentacles is a serious and studious gentleman, seeing many worlds in his sign.

Bill is certainly that and, when we met, he most certainly was a man with much money, all in change!

Knowing what the cards mean is the beginning. The next chapter tells us how to put our new knowledge to use and explains the art of divination with the Tarot.

CHAPTER NINE

The Past, the Present, and the Future

When you have at your fingertips a knowledge of what the cards mean, you are about to begin the next step in reading the Tarot. Take the deck into your hands and slowly, with an easy, rhythmic motion, shuffle them. Although the Tarot cards are bigger than most playing cards, practice will make it possible for you to handle them easily. When you shuffle the Tarot cards, concentrate on your question. As you know, the person who asks the question of the cards is called the _Querent;_ the person who will read and interpret the spread is called the _Reader._ When you have shuffled the cards thoroughly, pull three cards at random; don't look at them; replace them in the deck _reversed._ Now, with your left hand, in the old gypsy tradition, cut the deck into three — ▮ R To L piles. Shuffle each pile for a few moments from your right hand into your left hand; then, put them all back together again in one pile. _The cards are ready._

There are many different ways to lay out a spread. The possibilities run into the thousands! Now, we will concentrate on two simple and varied methods. Both are old and time honored. The first spread was taught to me in England by a wise woman. When she laid the cards out in this simple arrangement, the future became clear as a bell and all that was about to happen became apparent. Following Diagram A below, place the cards on a table or on the floor, as you wish, putting the cards in position according to the numbers in the diagram.

Each card, in its numbered position, represents a different part of your life—the past, the present, and the future. Keep the reference pages handy for interpretation, and let us see what you have unveiled.

Choose a Court card to represent the Querent; keep it in mind; then, leave it buried in the pack. Now, turn over the first card. Lay the cards down, one after another, following Diagram A. The positions mean the following:

1. The atmosphere that has existed in the Querent's life up to the present time. This card represents the way things have been.
Example: The Ten of Cups turns up as the first card. This means that a happy marriage, fruitful bliss, or a successful partnership of some kind is the atmosphere that you dwell in. If you are single, this card could tell that you dream of a happily married state continually. If married, here is your happy home. If things have been "on the rocks," here is the longed-for bliss

DIAGRAM A

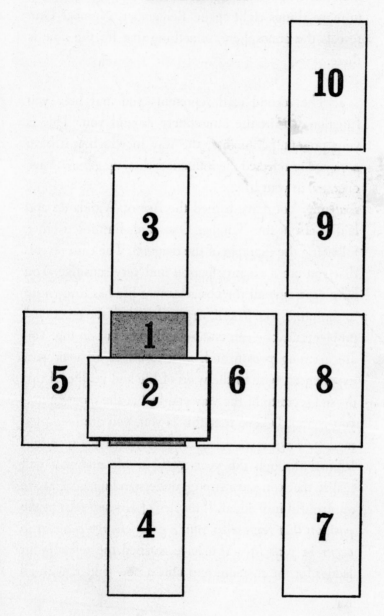

that you would attain, your daily and constant desire to make things right again. Remember, Number One reveals the atmosphere, something that for the *now* is there.

2. The second card represents you and how you function within the atmosphere around you. This is your present personality, the way in which you have accepted or rejected the influences that, up to now, have operated in your life.

Example: You have turned the Ace of Wands up and laid it across the Number One card, forming a cross, following the example of the diagram. The card reveals that you are a creative person and very sensitive. You have overcome all the obstacles that life has thrown up to confound you. You have weathered all the emotional problems anyone can endure and come out on top. You are a strong person and, as a result of all your past experiences, wise in the ways of life and people. If this doesn't seem to fit the way you feel at the moment and you cannot believe that this is you, you are being too modest. Take a close look at what you have seen and learned through the years of your life and you will realize that you are a strong, understanding, and, above all, fruitful individual. *If an Ace of any suit falls in the position that represents you, a great change is about to occur in your life.* You have reached the top of your ladder for the moment and now a new ladder, with all its problems and joys, is about to offer itself to you. The card that falls in this position is very important, no matter which one of the seventy-eight cards it is. This card represents you. You are seeing yourself!

3. Placed above the two central cards, Number Three represents the forces in your conscious reactions to the situations of your life, the forces in your highest and most-hoped-for dreams and ambitions. This card shows what you have and are striving for, where you think you want to go in life.

Example: The Ten of Swords falls in this position. Sad? Not at all. You have endured much misery and you want to change things and soon! You feel that nothing more can happen to you. You are at the bottom and the only way out is up. And you will climb. You are a strong person, remember, and all that you have been through has made you stronger. You may be very unhappy for the moment, perhaps you have gone out of your way to bring on unhappiness by becoming involved in a situation that seems hopeless and endless in its drain on your emotions. You have consciously brought on this unhappy state of mind and you can very easily, by realizing what you are, change all your sniffles into smiles.

Whatever card falls in this position, its message to you is—check your conscious actions and examine what you have gained on the path you have chosen. If a Court card pops up in this important position, it is quite possible that you have put your whole self into being like someone else, probably a loved one. The Tarot gives a deep and profound message here. To give and to love is wonderful and man's greatest experience, but . . . loving is one thing, becoming the shadow or carbon copy of the beloved is another. If that person should pass out of your life, you will be left devoid of personality, your identity gone. Examine the card in this position carefully and give much thought to the interpretation, for yourself and for others. This position is one of two vital keys to the future. The second key is the next card.

4. Number Four is placed below the two central cards. It represents your unconscious mind, that which motivates you and of which you may be unaware. Number Four is the foundation of your personality. It represents the inner force that controls all your actions. This card tells what is beneath the surface, the unconscious. It only represents a part of the intricate maze of your personality, but surely it will give a strong insight into the whys of your past and present, and indicate a guide to what the future will hold for you.

Example: If the Court card Strength falls in this position, you have a great power locked deep inside that sustains you through thick and thin. If you are female and Strength falls in the fourth position, your strength lies in your femininity. You have endured pain, perhaps childbirth; you have kept a "stiff upper lip" through lean years and through the problems of marriage. If you are single, you may be working hard to hold the budget and yourself together. But you are strong. You are naturally brave. You may be afraid, but you don't let it show. If you are a man, you realize subconsciously that gentleness can be strength but you don't really think about it consciously, you just go ahead and act with gentle strength; although it may surprise you, people respond positively. This card is vitally important. It represents part of the mind and its workings.

Perhaps the Two of Swords has fallen in this position. On the surface you appear well balanced and adjusted but that odd feeling of walking on the razor's edge seems to creep in now and then. What does it mean? It means simply that, deep inside, you are afraid. Of what? Think about it. Could it be that sometime, long ago, you did something you really should not have done and passed it off as foolishness? Because of your strict upbringing, you have always felt (not necessarily to your knowledge, but still *felt*) guilty and have been waiting for the "hand of retribution" to punish you. Silly? You would be surprised! Once you realize why you do things, then you can guide your life by your own hand. Position Number Four tells why you worry, why you love, why you hate, why you are pushing for a particular goal, and why you do or do not succeed. Check this card closely. Examine all its possible meanings and the variations on that meaning. Take a close look at what you are told; don't resent or deny any negative things that may show up. The wisdom of the Tarot will guide your future as it is shown to you and, if you follow the basic advice, only the very best of everything will come to you.

5. The fifth card, in position to the left of the central cards, represents the influences present in your life now that will be passing away shortly. It is the last card of the present.

Example: The Two of Cups falls in this position. Perhaps you have just become engaged or have just exchanged vows and promises of love with another. If you have just met someone attractive, you will certainly become very close to him in a short period of time. If things remained constant and did not change they would eventually stagnate, just like a pool of water that does not move. No matter how happy you may be at the moment, remember that no matter what this card denotes, *it is going to change.* If a Court card shows in this position, the person represented is going to cause a change in your life. Your response to that change is predicated on how you responded in the past to situations and how much you have learned about yourself and your responses to people and situations in the present. Whether people or events turn out for better or worse is up to you. The temporary state of affairs disclosed by this card gives you a chance to apply the teachings of the cards and can make for a much more enjoyable life in the future. The Tarot teaches that the only thing constant is change. You cannot make anyone or anything stay the same. The future of the situation expressed by this card shows up in the next card.

6. Number Six represents the immediate future. The time involved is shown by the number of the card. The higher the number on the card, the sooner the event will happen. An Ace means that the event will occur with great impact, a Court or Trump card relates the event to a particular person and also denotes impact and immediacy. Only the smaller cards—say Six through Two—denote a prolonged passage of time. Days are represented by Cups near Pentacles, weeks by Wands, and months by Swords, years by Pentacles. If a Court or Trump card falls in this position check the cards near it. If a Pentacles card is near any of these impact cards, it usually means that this event has been coming to a head for many years. If there are many Pentacles laid out, so far, and the Six card is also a Pentacle, the situation denoted may last for the number of years on the Six card.

Example: The Ace of Pentacles falls in this position. This is a powerful prophecy. One may expect the birth of a child who will bring great joy. It may mean that something long desired may be purchased during the winter months; there will be great abundance of money and material possessions. There will be ecstacy in the face of love and beauty, but, beware, greed can spoil everything. There is the thought that a project long cherished and planned for is about to come to a finish. Assuredly, there will be a culmination to something. What that thing or event may be, should already be explained by the previous cards. The immediate future opens a new door to a new experience. However, the Querent must examine his reactions and the emotional stirrings caused by what the Reader foresees. Let us assume that a negative card pops up, the Nine of Swords for example. Can there be any joy in a future promising sorrow, perhaps even sickness? Remember the wisdom of the cards once again. Situations are turned into problems only if they are looked upon as problems. Tears are just so much wasted energy unless we learn from our grief. Sorrow is necessary. The negative part of life stays with us just as long as we need it to give us an understanding of ourselves and others. Then the time to apply that understanding comes and, though the situation may stay the same, our reaction to the situation should change. Things may be at their worst and we may still be happy, knowing that the ability to cope is there and that we are learning a lesson. If a positive card should fall in this position, wonderful! Learn the lesson of this gift of sunshine; when the rain comes again, there will be new strength to understand and endure.

7. This card is placed at the bottom of the column we are building at the right. It is the first of four cards of the future. Number Seven represents the Querent in the environment of the future, his reactions and the way he will respond.

Example: Let us assume that the Queen of Cups appears here. If the Querent is female, there is no doubt that she is happy in her role of wife and mother. If the Querent is single, she will still enjoy a fruitful period in her work, being very productive and receiving appreciation from her coworkers. For the unwed, it holds a prophecy of marriage. If this card does not seem to represent the Querent herself, there will be a woman entering the Querent's life who will bear these characteristics and will play such an important role that her influence will predominate the Querent's daily existence. If a man finds this card so placed, there is the possibility that he will marry such a woman, or, if engaged, his future wife will turn out to be such a person. This position is also important because it tells how the Querent will respond to the preceding card (telling of a new turn of events). Examine Number Seven very closely.

8. This next card, in the column being built to the right, represents the important situations that will arise in the future and surround the Querent. The card denotes his *house* or the atmosphere in which he will live

91

and how these surrounding influences will affect the Querent.

Example: In this position, suppose we find the Court card, the Tower. Referring to the text, we see that this card foretells catastrophe. We also are told that, through this impending "purging," all unnecessary and detrimental forces that have operated in the Querent's life, up to the present, will be cast out. The card tells us that troubles and negative impact are coming to the end of their role in the Querent's life. The card falling in the eighth position, house or environment, always denotes a change from old established ways to new, fresh beginnings. Whatever the change is, it is always for the better. If by chance the Tower should be the card in this important position, all is not lost and the whole world is not going to come crashing down around the Querent's feet. It means simply that what has become unnecessary for growth—lost its usefulness or is detrimental to the Querent's evolution as an aware and productive person—is going to leave the Querent's life. Usually, when such situations occur, they are followed or surrounded by explosive upheaval. This is not something to feel sad about or to fear. Having become attached to some of these people or situations, their loss may cause grief. But no matter how much we may want to hang on, useless people, events, and attitudes are always replaced by something three times as good and valuable. The profound wisdom of the Tarot once again speaks the deepest truth. If we surround our lives with the old and useless and do not make way for inevitable change, we, ourselves, cannot grow or gain new wisdom. The new is always a challenge that should be met happily and with anticipation. The new atmosphere, denoted by the card falling in this position, should be examined for all its possibilities and messages, giving a great insight into the future.

9. The ninth card placed, according to the diagram, in the right-hand column represents the hopes and fears of the Querent. These desires will come as a result of future situations as foretold by the preceding cards. These are not realities, they are thoughts that will cross the Querent's mind in the time to come. At present, it may seem inconceivable that the Querent would wish for or be afraid of whatever the card foretells. The future is another story. Study this card well. It will give further clarity to the story of what tomorrow holds and the effect that the future will have on the Querent.

Example: The Four of Wands has fallen in this position. In the future, the Querent will dream of a large country home. He will envision the peace and quiet of the trees and the green earth, and hope for relaxation enabling him to think deep, poetic thoughts as he dwells within the glory of nature. The Reader will learn from this card that there will be adequate funds available to the Querent to allow him to purchase such a home. It will also become clear that the desire for such a home will give added impetus to the Querent's work, so that he may earn this wealth.

If negative cards have been the pattern of the past, it is possible that this dream will not come true because the Querent is unable to understand himself, to apply his talents, and there may possibly be destructive elements in the Querent's nature that put a stop to his spiritual and material growth. If this is the case, it is necessary for the Reader to apply the teachings of the Tarot to the explanation of the spread. The Reader should advise the Querent, in a considerate manner, that if he or she will set aside these useless old patterns, the future will be a bright, productive, new world. The dream of a large country estate can come true with application of the Querent's intelligence; nothing is impossible unless it is *not* attempted.

It may be that the other cards in the spread have foretold much material success for the Querent. The wish card is further verification of wealth to come. The fear that this dream will not come to pass is little more than the Querent's lack of faith in himself. The Reader should explain that, once the right path for any individual is chosen and that person comes to understand himself, there is very little that cannot be accomplished and gained.

It is also necessary for the Reader to understand that the card which falls in this position may be one of the

Querent's deepest fears in time to come. The reason for the presence of fear should be explained by the other cards and an analysis of the Querent's personality, as explained by the preceding cards. Perhaps, as in the case of the Four of Wands, the Querent fears the isolation of a large country house. If the Querent is a woman, it is possible that she is afraid of being left alone by her husband and having little contact with the busy city life.

10. This final card, placed at the top of the right-hand column, foretells what will come. It is the future, the outcome of all the circumstances previously described by the cards. When this event will occur is denoted by the suit and number of the card. If a Court card turns up, this event will occur with impact. The suit of the card beneath it (Number Nine) will disclose the time element. If that card is also a Court card, keep going back until a card of one of the four suits is found. The more Court cards near one another, the stronger the impact of the event. If you have decided to make the spread apply to the events of the coming month or two months, the last card will denote the end of that period of time and the date of the month in question. We'll detail that technique in Chapter Sixteen. Occasionally, the Reader may get the intuitive feeling that the events predicted by the last card will not occur for a longer period of time than the card denotes. When this hap-

pens, follow your intuition. The more you practice reading spreads, the faster your natural intuition will develop. Listen to your feelings. You will find that you are usually right. We all have the ability to feel things that are going to happen. Just as a baby must learn to walk by practice, so it is with intuition. It is a sense that must be developed with patience and much practice. The Tarot will help you to develop this sixth sense.

Example: If the last card to fall is the seven of Wands, the future holds success. Within seven weeks, the Querent will rise to a key position within his particular company or succeed greatly in his work. The card gives the warning—keep going whatever the enterprise; don't stop or hesitate or another will try to pass you on your journey to your goal. If a young man is the Querent and he is still a student, the indication is that competition is keen within the university; he must keep studying hard and he will have great success in examinations. The tenth card, in this position, is a completion of effort and resultant success. There is another message here. Life is a succession of cycles as we have already learned. Once something has been completed, the Querent has learned, from his journey to the top of this particular ladder, that wisdom gathered along the way must be applied to something new. The wisdom of the Tarot says simply: now that you have reached a completion point, do not think of yourself as one who can stop and toss away what you have learned; do not rest on your laurels. A new cycle is about to begin. The most important message here is to reflect upon the big and little incidents of the past. What have you learned about yourself and others? How can you apply that knowledge to your new set of circumstances? Remember also the great truth that all things change. You will not remain in status quo. You may be on top now but within a new cycle you will rise or fall. If you fall it is for growth, and you have more lessons to learn. If you rise higher, it is because you have learned your lessons well. You will have setbacks. Then, you must look into your storehouse of knowledge and understand why these events are happening and learn still another lesson in this new cycle. Push ahead and continue your climb to the very best expression of your own private and individual personality.

CHAPTER TEN

The Gypsy Method of Tarot Reading

Although we have already presented one of the easiest yet most effective methods of laying out a spread, it is certain that the occasion will arise when the Querent will want a more thorough explanation of his past, present, and future. Diagram B describes another method of divination with the Tarot cards. It is more detailed and a bit more complicated. Once you have become adept in reading the cards with the first method, this second method, long used by the wandering gypsies of eastern Europe, will prove simple to master and fascinating. The gypsy method is an excellent way to clarify unanswered questions following the ten-card reading (described in the previous chapter).

Have the Querent reshuffle the entire pack in the prescribed manner explained at the beginning of Chapter Nine. When the cards are shuffled and cut, the Reader then asks the Querent to count off thirty-five cards, beginning with the top card of the pack. These cards are counted off into one pack; the remaining cards

DIAGRAM B

PACKETS

1	2	3	4	5	6

PACKET

#1. ☐☐☐☐☐☐☐☐ -7 cards

#2. ☐☐☐☐☐☐☐ -6 cards

#3. ☐☐☐☐☐☐ -5 cards

#4. ☐☐☐☐☐ - 4 cards

#5. ☐☐☐ - 2 cards

#6. ☐☐☐☐☐☐☐☐☐☐☐ -11 cards

are set aside. The Querent again shuffles and cuts the pack of thirty-five cards and returns the pack to the Reader. The cards are now divided into six packets which are dealt out, face down, as follows:

Packet 1, the first seven cards; Packet 2, the next six cards; Packet 3, the next five cards; Packet 4, the next four cards; Packet 5, the next two cards; Packet 6, the last eleven cards.

Set the packets next to each other as in the diagram. Take up the packets, one at a time, and deal out each one, face up in a line, one line under the other, making six lines of unequal length, following Diagram B. Each packet has its own line and each line represents something important to the Querent's life.

The First Line—represents the atmosphere of the present. The cards in this line should define the elements of the past and the present that have gone in to creating the existing house or environment.

The Second Line— represents the Querent or the subject matter that is being discussed. This could be a business enterprise, a relationship, or a person that the Reader wishes to clarify further for the Querent. A Court card in this line may represent the Querent or the party whom the Querent wishes to know more about. This line deals with the personality and the makeup of the Querent or of the person or of the situation in question.

The Third Line—represents the outside influences operating around the Querent, situation, or event in question. These are influences that the Querent has no control over and which affect him or the situation through forces created by others, not by the Querent. A very important line, it tells the Querent what others are doing for or against him or his situation. Through the Tarot, he will find the answers that will enable him to turn these influences to his advantage.

The Fourth Line—represents the unexpected. This line further defines what will happen in the immediate future in the form of surprises so that the Querent may prepare for them ahead of time.

The Fifth Line—is the line of consolation, or the silver lining to any dark clouds that may have appeared in the preceding lines. Herein lie the most profound cards of wisdom. By supplying the Querent with the wisdom of each card in this line, the Reader can turn the unhappiness of the past into understanding for the Querent. This line teaches the Querent how to cope with what is coming and what has happened. It also tells of what will come in the form of joy to replace losses and unhappiness.

The Sixth Line—is a preview of the events surrounding the future. The previous ten-card run ended with one card of the future. This line goes on to explain all the possibilities of that future card. This is also a wisdom line. Each card holds a deep message for the Reader to understand and translate for the Querent. The gypsies have called this line the Death line or the line of the future, that which is unknown and now revealed.

These cards should be read from left to right beginning with the top line.

Example: In the first line of seven cards you turn up the following cards in sequence: the Ace of Cups, Two of Swords, King of Pentacles, Queen of Cups, the Fool, Ten of Cups, the Four of Pentacles.

The first line represents the house or the environment of the Querent. Knowing this and applying the meanings of the cards in sequential order, we would be able to determine the following information. The Ace of Cups denotes a strong element of love surrounding the Querent. The Two of Swords offers the information that, although the Querent is happy in his home or environment, an element of suspense prevails. The next card is the King of Pentacles so we may assume that the tension in the environment is a result of the King's presence. This card may denote that the Querent, if a male, is creating this tension himself. If the Querent is a woman, a man who plays a prominent part in her life, a King of Pentacles type, is causing the distress. Because the following card is the Queen of Cups, we then learn that a relationship between the King and the Queen has brought about the tension. This can be a husband-wife relationship, a friendship, or perhaps an extramarital affair between the husband, represented by the King, and another woman, represented by the Queen. As the next card is the Fool, the indication is that the Queen is a nonconformist and attractive to the King because she lacks responsible traits. The next card in sequence is the Ten of Cups, which denotes a happy marriage. Should the King and Queen represent husband and wife rather than a person or persons outside of the marriage, the influence of the two of Swords will lift, and harmony will be restored. Should the King or Queen denote someone outside of the home, that person's influence will end, the tension will lift, and the happy marriage will be restored. The next card, the Four of Pentacles denotes a legacy or an inheritance and warns the Querent to hold tightly to what he or she has. The Four of Pentacles card in this position would denote money coming into the home, resolving financial problems that very possibly could have caused the tension between the King and the Queen. It is not unusual, where there are financial difficulties, for a happily married couple to find themselves "at war" with one another. Quite often, to escape the tensions within the home, one of the parties loses sight of his marital obligations and becomes involved with another person for a brief period of time.

The situation is not a permanent but a temporary escape from the responsibilities of marriage and financial obligations. If the marriage has a good, solid foundation, as denoted by the Ace of Cups and the Ten of Cups, the problem is temporary and should be treated with understanding. When financial pressure moves into a marriage, a partner may search for escape from responsibility in a relationship with an irresponsible person; the partner chooses someone who does not worry over finances and envies the person. The situation is always temporary and, if taken in its proper perspective, the marriage will be strengthened by the realization that the other partner is understanding though not appreciative of the spouse's actions. When the marriage scales become balanced once again, through self-understanding, the incident and the person involved are reduced to their proper proportions and disappear from the picture.

The second line represents the Querent and offers further information regarding the Querent's personality traits or the traits and possibilities of the subject or situation under consideration.

Example: In the second line, the six cards in order of appearance are: the Ace of Wands, the Tower, the Ten of Swords, the Six of Cups, the Hermit, and the Hanged Man. The inherent traits revealed through these cards offer further analysis of the Querent's personality or the subject or situation under scrutiny. The presence of the

Ace of Wands in this position denotes that the person involved is talented; there is an indication of inventiveness and fertility on all planes of endeavor. If a situation rather than a particular person is involved, the creation of something is denoted; the situation is powerful and important to the Querent but can be lost through too many drives which negate the completion of any one thing.

The Tower, as the next card, would suggest that the Querent is undergoing a period of depression resulting from the destruction of established ideas and the crumbling of prestige or position resulting from plans that were built on a faulty foundation.

The Ten of Swords, which follows, would denote misery and unhappiness over this situation making the Querent melancholy and filled with woe.

Next, the Six of Cups would denote that the Querent is lost in dreams of the past. There is an indication here that the Querent is given to daydreaming. If the daydreaming is along constructive lines, it is possible that he will benefit from his past mistakes and bring about the necessary changes to rebuild his personality, his business, his marriage, or whatever is under consideration, in a constructive and positive manner.

The Hermit denotes a seeker, one who values wisdom over the more material things of life. This is a good card here as it gives the Reader an insight into the Querent's personality so that advice of a deep and profound nature may be directed toward the Querent and will be understood or applied. If a specific situation is involved rather than a human personality, the situation will be of a philosophical nature, something pertaining to learning and deep thought, perhaps the Querent's involvement with a person of this nature or the development of a project involving a school or a religious or philosophical institution.

The last card, the Hanged Man, denotes a tendency toward self-sacrifice and the putting forth of unselfish energies in connection with people or projects. A lack of conformity to the established rules of society is indicated, placing the Querent or the situation in an "upside-down" position. The Querent should be advised that some constructive selfishness and consideration of his role in the situation could lead to greater success. It may also be stressed here that, if the Querent follows a more conventional course, it will be easier to influence others to his way of thinking.

Looking at the line as a whole, there is a definite artistic or creative part to the personality of the Querent or situation. The indications of undirected energies, developed creative ability, nonconformity, and general daydreaming on the part of the Querent should be brought to the Querent's attention; constructive advice can be given in relation to these areas. Rechecking the first line against the second would denote that these creative problems have led to financial difficulties and involvements with artistic and unconventional people outside the Querent's married life.

Each line can be easily interpreted by evaluating the individual cards. It is then up to the Reader to incorporate all the information and to draw a total picture for the Querent. When this is accomplished it is then necessary for the Reader to advise, using the wisdom of the cards, so that the Querent may be guided in the best possible paths for his happiness and growth and for the happiness and growth of those intimately involved with him.

The greatest problem the Reader will have to face is a person's inability to recognize his own faults and to blame circumstances on everyone but himself. It should be pointed out to the Querent that a person attracts and chooses to put into his life pattern only those things he really wants, whether he chooses on a conscious level or not. Having learned from the Tarot that history will repeat itself unless actions are checked and redirected, it is necessary for the Reader to point out the Querent's habit patterns, which always show up in the cards, and then to redirect valuable energies into positive, constructive paths. The fate of a man can be altered, since we each shape our own fate. Nothing happens by accident. We create all of our situations. We unconsciously punish ourselves for things that we feel we have done wrong. If there is a period of joy in our lives, we have given ourselves the opportunity to enjoy that period by the acceptance of ourselves and the acceptance of our deeds. This should be pointed out to the Querent so that in the future there will be less inclination toward self-punishment and the depression that results.

The remaining five lines should be interpreted with this same sort of detail and the same application of logic. The more you familiarize yourself with the individual cards, the easier it will be for you to give such detailed readings.

Because ordinary playing cards are the offspring of the Tarot, it is possible to foretell the future using a fifty-two-card pack. The meanings of the cards are similar to those of the Tarot, with a few differences. In the following chapter I will explain a method of divination with regular playing cards, give the meanings of each card and a diagram for laying out a spread. The Tarot, which is the basis for these ordinary cards, still provides the Reader and the Querent with great messages of wisdom in this other method of divination.

CHAPTER ELEVEN

Divination with Standard Playing Cards

The situation may arise when, for one reason or another, you do not have a pack of Tarot cards on hand. Perhaps you are away from home and a companion comes to you with a problem he is wrestling with. You know that the Tarot eventually became the ordinary playing cards; once you have learned the meanings of these fifty-two cards, it is possible to give a wise reading. The interpretation of a spread of standard playing cards is similar to a Tarot spread but the Tarot cards are more exact. There are a few variations. The two most important differences are the absence of the Knight in each suit and the absence of the Court cards or the first twenty-two symbol-pictures. The Jack is both the Page and the Knight in each suit. The sex of the Jack is determined by the direction in which the Jack's eyes point. The age of the Jack is always younger than the King or the Queen. The meaning of each Jack will be carefully explained so you may determine without difficulty, the age, sex, and personality of the person represented. The Court cards eventually became incorporated into the various number cards of each suit. The Fool became the Joker, the Hermit became the Ten of Diamonds, and the Tower became the Nine of Spades.

The suits—Hearts, Clubs, Spades, and Diamonds—were originally Cups, Wands, Swords, and Pentacles. If we take a broad look at the history of divination with playing cards, we find that the basic meanings of these ordinary cards have not changed with time. Each country draws its face cards with an original flair and presents the number cards in the suits with artistic variations. No matter how pretty or different in appearance your deck of standard playing cards may appear, this difference has no bearing whatsoever on the meaning of each card.

There are literally thousands of different ways to lay out a spread with ordinary cards. The method illustrated below is simple and always proves accurate. When it was first presented to me in England many years ago, I was astounded at how simply and truthfully my own and my friends' problems came to light. This method can be used to read one's own and anyone else's cards.

Diagram C shows the positions of the cards in the spread. Each card represents a new facet of the Querent's personality and of the present and future situations and problems.

To begin, take an ordinary bridge deck and remove one of the Jokers; leave just one Joker in the pack. You

DIAGRAM C

12	8	4			5	9	13
		3	1	2			
15	11	7		6	10	14	

are now using fifty-three cards. Without breaking the deck, shuffle the cards with an easy, rhythmic motion. Keep shuffling until the cards are well mixed and they "feel right." Now give the pack to the Querent and let him repeat the shuffle. While the Querent is handling the cards, clear all thoughts from your mind, then concentrate on the Querent silently, for wisdom and intuition in reading the spread. Imagine a circle upon the table or floor where the cards will be spread and picture the cards as the center of the circle. The reading should be held in a place away from other people and away from interruptions such as the telephone or the doorbell. Now, advise the Querent to cut the pack into three piles and to shuffle each pile into his right hand with his left hand. Tell the Querent to make a wish while shuffling the cards and to concentrate on that wish. The Reader should have no knowledge of the Querent's wish. The cards will tell what the Querent is thinking. After each of the three piles are shuffled, the Querent should put the packs together in one pile. The pack is handed back to the Reader who now begins to lay out the spread according to Diagram C. When using ordinary cards, no card is reversed. A reversed meaning is found only in the Tarot cards.

With all fifteen cards laid out in their proper positions (Diagram C) the Reader now begins to concentrate on the spread. Each card is influenced by the cards adjacent to it. There should be no comment on any card until the entire spread is down. Put the remainder of the pack aside and concentrate. The positions of the cards in the spread shown on Diagram C have the following meanings:

1—The card represents the Querent or his personality and the nature of his problems. These are the most important influences moving through his life at the present time.

2—3—These cards on either side of the central card clarify the nature of the central card. They represent information regarding the situation of the Querent. If the central card describes the Querent himself, the two cards in these positions go on to describe this person in more elaborate detail. If the central card is a face card of the sex opposite to the Querent, this card usually represents someone who plays a central and dominant role in the Querent's life. A card showing a person of the same sex, but unlike the Querent in nature, usually represents a person of the same sex who is extremely important in the Querent's life—a mother, father, or friend.

4—8—12—These three cards in the upper right wing represent the Querent's normal course, unless some action is taken to stop the flow of events. This wing also represents what will happen to the Querent in his situation but leaves an alternate path if the cards show a bad ending to the natural path.

13—9—5—The three cards in the upper left wing

show an alternate route that the Querent may pursue. These possibilities may be better than the natural path. The cards will show which route is more desirable. The end card of each of these upper wings shows whether or not the path ends well or badly. Often, difficult cards end well and the more joyous cards end in a wall or barrier or perhaps disappointment. Each wing should be carefully examined for alternative choices.

14—10—16—The three cards in the lower left wing are messages of wisdom pertaining to the Querent's situation, which should guide him in making his decisions. When the Querent is elderly or past middle age, this wing often represents past influences or experiences which should be taken into consideration before a move in the present is made. If the Querent is youthful, these cards denote future events and offer a method of preparing for what will come.

7—11—15—The three cards in the lower right wing represent forces which are presently operating outside of the Querent's control. By being made aware of what is going on around him, the Querent may be able to turn some of these situations to his own advantage.

As the reader becomes more proficient at reading the cards, certain individual cards may take on a special meaning to him. This is a common and standard event. As the gypsies say "the oracle speaks to each diviner in a separate tongue."

The position in which the card falls varies its meaning. In the following text of interpretations, a meaning is given for each card according to its position in the spread.

THE JOKER—The Joker was originally the Fool of the Tarot. The Tarot interpretation of this card applies here. When the Joker is found in the middle of the spread it denotes that the Querent is, to some degree, this type of person. He wishes independence from social conventions, has a desire for great wisdom, and has rid himself of petty problems and jealousies. He has, to some extent, risen above tragedy, misery, and conflict to find a unity of mind and spirit. The other cards will explain the manner in which the Querent has applied this wisdom, or in some cases misused it.

In the upper wings, the Joker foretells that the Querent will be caught in a situation of choice. He may have to reject the spiritual freedom he desires in order to attain material success, or he may have to accept the restrictions of material possessions and the rules of society in order to succeed socially.

In the lower wings, the Joker represents a situation where the Querent may have the opportunity to act on his high ideals or may have to compromise his beliefs for profit or in a social situation.

CHAPTER TWELVE

The Suit of Clubs

ACE—In the center of the spread, the Ace of Clubs denotes great talent within the Querent. This indicates artistic talent, intuition, the ability to express one's self through writing, art, music, the theater, or perhaps through the church as a minister. There is a warning that too many drives may result in the accomplishment of nothing. The Querent is prone to a fantasy existence which can hold him in a world of dreams; however inspiring, such a life gives no concrete results in terms of production.

This card, when found in any of the wings, denotes either an opportunity to use this talent, this talent being present in another if it falls next to a face card representing another person, or success for the Querent as a result of this ability. The surrounding cards will tell where and when this talent will prove important in the Querent's life.

TWO—This card denotes a social invitation. In the center of the spread, the invitation will play a very important role in the Querent's life. If next to a face card of the opposite sex, a romantic situation could well result from the acceptance of this invitation.

In any of the wings, the surrounding cards should be examined to see what the outcome of accepting the invitation will bring. If in a wing that ends with a block or a card of tears and misery, it is better that the Querent ignore the invitation. If the card falls at the end of any of the wings this invitation will be the outcome of the situations described by the cards next to the two.

THREE—The card denotes an unpleasant social incident. If the three falls in the center of the spread it is possible that the Querent's reaction to this snub, gossip, or insult will be out of proportion to the intent behind the episode.

In any of the wings, this situation will be minor. If next to a face card, the nature and source of the incident will be apparent. How the situation should be handled and the objective method of turning the incident to the Querent's benefit will be explained by the other cards in the wing. The indication here is that the Querent may handle an unpleasant situation with kindness and understanding and consequently make a right out of a wrong. If tempers are lost and bitterness and vindictiveness result, everyone involved will be hurt. This is a minor episode and should be treated as such.

FOUR—This card denotes that the Querent is held in high regard by those around him and if made aware of this respect and cherishing, the Querent can strengthen his friendships and social activities. If found in the center of the spread, the indication is that in time of need the Querent may call upon others to help him and will receive this help immediately. If the Querent is unhappy and lonely, he should be advised that this is all in his imagination and that with a little show of warmth he will be surrounded by friends who have held him in high regard for a long time.

In any of the wings, this card indicates that a situation will arise or end up in such a way that the friendship of others will play an important role in his life. The friendship is there for the asking; if the Querent shows overt appreciation of others, they will gladly come to his aid. There is also an indication here that the Querent underestimates himself and does not feel that he is capable of inspiring friendship and loyalty in others. The Reader should tell the Querent that this feeling of inadequacy is false and advise him to make an effort to uncover admirable traits in his friends and associates.

FIVE—The Five of Clubs denotes that a quarrel may cause a separation of dear friends. The quarrel is between the Querent and one of his own sex. If a face card of the opposite sex lies next to the five, it can then denote a difference of opinion between man and woman. If the card falls in the middle of the spread it denotes rivalry, competition, and jealousy of the success of others. Whether the Querent or someone else starts the argument, the end result is the important factor. This card, appearing in the middle of the spread, warns of serious aftereffects unless the Querent treats the situation with objectivity and wisdom and acts with kindness, consideration, and, most of all, understanding of the other person's motives.

If the Five is in the upper wings, the quarrel may be avoided by consulting the adjacent cards about how to guide the Querent away from an unnecessary and potentially sorry situation.

In the lower wings, the quarrel relates to the specific situation described by the other cards. It is possible, when the card is in the lower wings, that another's ill-will could cause disappointment in a once-promising social situation. The best method to handle the situation is described by the cards around the Five. It is very possible that a seeming loss of prestige can have a good end result. Check the cards near the Five for the outcome.

SIX—In the center of the spread, the Six denotes a flowering social life. There is an indication of popularity and many social engagements. The happiness involved here may relate to increased growth of mind and spirit as a result of new contacts and the increased appreciation and understanding of others.

In the wings, this card retains its basic meaning. If it

is an end card in any of the wings, there will be a period of happy and fruitful recreation after a period of dormant social activities. It may also be the end result of a meeting with a person of the opposite sex, if a face card lies next to the Six.

SEVEN—In the center of the spread, the Seven tells of a person who has high aspirations but does not complete a task once it is started. It tells of the need for hard work and effort to accomplish a goal.

In the upper left wing, the Seven indicates that the Querent is seeking a goal attainable only through diligent work and effort. The Querent should be warned against giving into self-doubt and resigning himself to failure.

In the upper right wing, there is a danger of loss through neglect. This position warns against taking things for granted.

In the lower wings, the card denotes a specific situation which the Querent is involved in but which is being supervised by others. There is a danger of carelessness on the part of employees or associates. The Querent should be cautioned against disclosing plans to others and against announcing premature success.

EIGHT—The Eights are all cards of balance. The Eight of clubs denotes emotional balance, harmony with nature, and a delight in peace and beauty. In the center of the spread the card indicates a balanced personality, a person who has a clear recognition of values and a realization of the important things of life. The Eight of clubs in any spread is fortunate. This ability to understand and appreciate the important things of life will guard the Querent from the constant emotional ups and downs of daily living.

In any of the wings the card remains similar in meaning. If next to a face card, the Querent will meet such a person and learn from him. If the Eight is the end card in any of the wings, the card denotes a fine outcome to the present problems of the Querent's life. The ability to cope with and understand all his difficult situations will come to the Querent.

NINE—The Nine of Clubs represents success and accomplishment in one's work. It also denotes stability, emotional adjustment, and progress. It can mean that a work of art is completed and sold or that a business contract is signed.

In the upper wings, the success will depend on the immediate actions of the Querent. Opportunity is within reach. The steps to accomplishment should be outlined by the other cards in the wing.

In the lower wings, the card denotes a specific situation which can bring the Querent success, fame, and money.

TEN—The Ten represents a young person whose life

is linked with the Querent's. In the older Querent, the card may be a grandchild, son, or daughter. In the younger Querent, it may be a friend. This card is not the Querent but someone through whom the Querent will find inspiration and who will awaken new or forgotten interests. In any position in the spread this card suggests new ideas, new interests, and fresh patterns which will add to the Querent's life. The person represented in the card should be defined by a face card near the ten.

JACK—Wherever the Jack appears in the spread, his personality remains the same. If the Jack's eyes point to the middle of the spread this young person will be the sex opposite to the Querent. If the eyes point away from the middle of the spread, the person will be the Querent's own sex. The Jack of Clubs is honest, sincere, and hard working. This person is devoted to the Querent. The Jack is often underestimated. He or she may be considered dull, naïve, unsophisticated, lacking in the social graces, or just plain drab. This evaluation is misleading. The Jack is loyal to the core and will come to the Querent's aid without hesitation. The Jack is often talented but, because he wants to put the Querent in the best possible light, he often conceals this talent and is content to be second best. The Jack may be resented because he shows little tact. Sometimes, in an outspoken way, he cautions the Querent against hasty action. He is naturally honest and is an invaluable friend. The presence of the Jack in the spread is an indication that the Querent has such a person in his life. Usually this person is not fully appreciated. The presence of the Jack also indicates that a situation may arise where the friendship of this person will be a tower of strength. The Querent should be warned against a one-sided relationship with this person and advised that greater consideration and appreciation is needed on his part to maintain this friendship.

QUEEN—The Queen of Clubs possesses the same personality traits as the Queen of Wands in the Tarot deck. The Queen of Hearts and the Queen of Clubs will be attracted to one another. The Queen of Spades is her instinctive enemy. If the Queen of Clubs and the Queen of Spades occur in the same spread, there is a strong indication of conflict. The Queen of Spades will win because of her greater subtlety and intuition.

In the center of the spread, the Queen of Clubs denotes the Querent's personality or the problems that the Querent is up against. If another Queen or Jack lies next to the Queen of Clubs in the center of the spread, the personality of the Queen of Clubs will take on the characteristics of the other face card and modify her basic personality.

The male Querent, who finds this card in the center of his spread, will have a dominant woman in his life with these character traits.

A Queen of Clubs in the upper wings is an indication that such a woman will soon enter the Querent's life and play an important role. If the Queen of Clubs falls in the upper left wing, the Querent may have to make a decision with regard to this woman.

In either of the lower wings, the indication is that appearances will be deceptive in a future situation. Snap judgments should be abandoned until the Querent has time to evaluate the situation objectively. In any position, if the nine of Hearts falls near this card, the meaning is that this woman will bring great joy into the Querent's life and be the fulfillment of his wish for happiness. (See Tarot interpretation of the Queen of Wands for further information.)

KING—The King of Clubs bears the personality and character traits of the King of Wands (see Tarot text). The Queen of Diamonds and the King of Clubs are made for each other. She will bring out his good points and further his talents and ambitions. If the King of Clubs becomes involved with the Queen of Spades, misery will certainly result. With her withdrawn manner and buried passions, the Queen of Spades will hold him back from success. If both cards appear in a spread there is an indication of a broken home, separation, and divorce. This is intensified if cards of quarrels or loss surround the King and Queen.

In the center of a female Querent's spread, the King of Clubs is an important and dominant person in her life. In the case of a male Querent, the card usually represents himself. In the wings, the King is a man who will be important in the Querent's life: a close friend, a relative, or a business associate. In the wings of a female Querent's spread, the King will come into her life in the future and play an important role. The nature of the activity will be described by the other cards in the wing.

CHAPTER THIRTEEN

The Suit of Diamonds

ACE—The Ace represents mathematical knowledge, engineering skill, and an interest in sciences such as biology, astronomy, biochemistry, archaeology, and architecture. The Ace also represents the acquisition of material wealth as the result of hard work. The Magician is likened to the Ace of Diamonds, and the interpretation of that Tarot card applies to this card in all its facets.

If the Ace appears in the upper left wing of the spread, it foretells an opportunity about to present itself to the Querent that he will do well to watch for and to turn to his advantage.

If the ace appears in the upper right wing, it means that the Querent has already embarked upon, or is in the planning stages of embarking upon, a venturous plan and will do so shortly. If the Two of Spades lies to the left of the Ace of Diamonds, there is a warning of delay. If the Ten of Spades lies to the right, the consideration of other plans would be the wisest move.

In the lower wings, the same powerful force is present whether it be an occurrence in the future in the left hand wing or a force acting outside of the Querent's knowledge.

TWO—In the middle of the spread, the Two foretells an unexpected communication concerning money or business. This may be an inheritance, a gift, or an opportunity for an advancement at work.

In any of the wings, the card denotes a minor, isolated experience, alien to the Querent's major life patterns. How the situation will end, or where the communication comes from, will be explained by the other cards in the spread.

THREE—This card represents a legal document. It can be anything from a business contract to a divorce decree or a marriage license. The card includes all types of legal, contractual agreements. The outcome will be described by the cards in the wings. This holds true in any position of the card in the spread.

FOUR—This card denotes success through diligent application in business, finance, and professional status. The Four does not change meaning in any position in the spread, although the cards surrounding the Four should be examined for further information regarding the nature of the success.

FIVE—The card foretells the clash of wills between two people or within a group of people. The conflict is not an outright fight but rather an unconscious clash of personalities or values. The Five has this meaning in any of the wings. In the center of the spread, it can also mean that the Querent is "at war" with himself and that in his activities he has two sets of opposing desires or sets of values that can lead to indecisiveness and hamper growth and success.

SIX—This is a card of well-being, physical comfort, and material security with money in the bank. In the center of the spread, it can denote the Querent's preoccupation with these matters.

In the upper wings, the position of the card denotes either an outcome of events leading to material security and peace of mind or denotes the obstacles that must be overcome in order to attain this position.

In the lower wings, the card foretells an opportunity to accomplish these ends; the surrounding circumstances are shown by the other cards in the wing.

SEVEN—The Seven denotes a problem, yet unresolved, that is weighing on the Querent. It may be a financial, a domestic, or, possibly, a business problem. The outcome of the problem or the remedy is shown by the surrounding cards.

If the Seven appears in the upper wings, the indication is that such a problem may arise but can be avoided.

If in the lower wings, the problem will involve the Querent indirectly. The problems of others may affect the Querent.

EIGHT—This is another balance card. It denotes financial skills and material success balanced by an appreciation of these things and of the spiritual part of life. It denotes an unselfish, fair person. It is the card of moderation.

In the upper wings, the indication is that a decision will have to be made where careful judgment is necessary. The situation in question will be defined by the other cards in the wing. If next to a face card, it may be necessary to discuss the situation with a person in authority to obtain additional information.

If the card is near many Clubs, the indication is that there will be steady gain, peace, and the absence of problems.

NINE—The Nine is the card of wish fulfillment. In the center of the spread, it denotes that the wish is of utmost importance to the Querent and will be fulfilled through the Querent's desire to accomplish his ends.

If the nine is in the upper wings, the Querent must change his life patterns and the wish will be fulfilled in the normal course of events.

In the lower wings, the Nine shows that the wish will be controlled by outside forces in the Querent's life. If the Nine falls at the end of a wing, the wish will be fulfilled after many delays and troubles. If the Nine does not appear, it does not deny the Querent his wish but does mean that no definite answer can be given at this time. If the Nine of Hearts is in the same spread as the Nine of Diamonds, the indication is that the Querent will experience happiness beyond all his expectations and beyond the perimeters of the wish.

TEN—The card denotes confinement or material bondage. It is the card of wealth that does not bring happiness. In the center of the spread there is an indication of cynicism, world-weariness, and acceptance of a life that lacks deeper significance. This holds true in the upper wings also. The Querent should be advised of the opportunities available to change his humdrum life, of ways to use his money to further his spiritual growth.

In the lower wings, the meaning changes and the card denotes a pleasurable interlude from everyday living. This may come through an inheritance, an opportunity to travel, or from an experience that will broaden the Querent's ideas and frame of reference. The opportunity must be taken, or boredom will move in and destroy the Querent's full enjoyment of life.

JACK—The Jack of Diamonds is the Hanged Man of the Tarot cards. The same definition applies. The sex is determined by the direction of the Jack's eyes (see Jack of Clubs). The Jack, anywhere in the spread, retains his personality. If in the upper right wing he or she will be coming into the Querent's life. In the middle of the spread, the Jack is the Querent or a person very important in his life. In the lower wings he again represents a person who will shortly enter the Querent's life. For further information check the cards surrounding the Jack.

QUEEN—The Queen of Diamonds is a bit more flamboyant than the Queen of Pentacles but retains the latter's basic personality. She is restless, constantly on the go, and she gets things accomplished. She is passionate and quick tempered, and is fond of the color red. The Queen of Pentacles or Diamonds and the Queen of Spades are dire enemies. She is "made in heaven" for the King of Clubs. In the center of the spread the Queen usually represents the Querent or someone very important in the Querent's life. If a male is the Querent and the Queen is in the center of the spread, she plays an important role in his life. It is wise to find the card representing the Querent and to decide whether the Querent will be able to establish a rapport with the Queen or, if possible, how the Querent will be affected by such a person in his or her life.

In the outer wings, she will be a person whom the Querent will meet and she will play an important role in his or her life.

KING—The King here is much like the King of Pentacles but a bit more mercurial in temperament and he is artistic, subtle, and intelligent. His temper is violent but his compassion is deep. His sensitivity can make him great or destroy him. Though he carries a facade of aggressiveness he can be easily hurt and needs someone to build his ego and bring out his good points. He is loyal to his family and friends but he is critical and occasionally sharp with his loved ones; in a "mood," he can easily hurt the ones he loves most; later he is apologetic and brings gifts or flatters the object of his affections. In the center of the spread this card usually represents the Querent or someone important in the Querent's life if the Querent is female.

In the upper wings, he represents someone who will enter the Querent's life shortly. This holds true in the lower wings but the Querent must decide whether such a person in his or her life spells happiness or disaster.

If the Querent is a woman and the King appears in the lower wings, she will not be able to hold this man no matter how hard she may try. If the Querent is a man, he must gauge his relationship with this King. If the King is a negative type, he may destroy all that the Querent has attempted to build for himself and his loved ones.

CHAPTER FOURTEEN

The Suit of Hearts

ACE—This card is the card of love. It denotes joy, happiness, and growth. If in the middle of the spread, love will be a part of the Querent's personality.

When the Ace is in the upper wings, it means that joy, love, and the sense of all being right with the world will come into the Querent's life. The manner and the people who may be involved with this love and happiness will be described by the other cards in the wing.

In the lower wings, the card means that the Querent is loved and cherished by another but does not realize this fact. He may even feel unloved.

In any position the card promises love, happiness, marriage, and children; the other cards in the wings describe the additional factors involved in the relationship. The people involved will be represented by face cards.

TWO—The card denotes a love letter or a piece of good news. The card does not change meaning in any position although the other cards should be examined to find out the source of this happiness and the outcome.

THREE—The card denotes a disappointment in love, a minor setback in plans, or an error in judgment. There is also an indication of self-delusion. The indication is that, if a change is made in the Querent's life as represented by the other cards in the wing, the situation of disappointment will lose proportion and the Querent will be able to grow in stature.

FOUR—In any position in the spread, the Four denotes an opportunity for happiness through work. This comes as a result of putting the interests of others before one's own desires. The cards in the wing further clarify this happiness and the source from which it will come. If in the center of the spread, the source is within the Querent's daily pattern of living.

FIVE—This card, in any position, represents disappointment, tears, and vain regret. It can be the end of a love affair or setting aside, because of interceding problems, the most desired plan that the Querent may have. The incident must be placed in proportion so that the Querent may make other, more solid plans for the future. It is important to notice that this sorrow is never a deep misery and will pass quickly, although in the present all may seem black and lost.

SIX—This card denotes the beginning of happiness, the first step toward success. The Querent must be warned against impatience.

In the middle of the spread, this card tells of a decision that will soon have to be made.

In the upper wings the meaning is the same, though in the left upper wing the choice is optional.

In the lower wings, the choice may or may not be made but will, if well taken, lead to a specific opportunity for happiness.

SEVEN—The card denotes a lover's quarrel. The Querent may be too quick to fly off the handle. He should examine his real thought before going off into a rage. Others may be unnecessarily hurt. Appearing in any of the wings, the card denotes that the Querent will suffer from loss if he does not watch his tongue. There are others much attached to the Querent who do not wish to see such a scene occur. The Querent may be shy and use anger to attract the attention he seeks. He should be advised that criticism, nagging, and hostility are not necessary to gain the affections of a beloved.

EIGHT—The card denotes a gift which causes pleasure. If it falls in the center of the spread there will be an exchange of gifts. It may be a gift of love.

In the upper wings the gift will have a deep meaning. The gift should not be treated lightly.

In the lower wings the gift may be a gift of service to another or, if in the lower wing to the left, it will have an intrinsic value and come from a source not directly related to the Querent.

If the Querent's reading tells of the need for caution, the card may represent a bribe which should be rejected at all costs.

NINE—In any position, the card represents happiness beyond all expectations. The wish that the Querent has made will be granted in a way least expected. This will bring enduring happiness. The presence of the Nine indicates self-awareness, inner joy, and a good future for the Querent.

TEN—In any position in the spread, the Ten represents a messenger who brings good news. Though this message may cause the upset of plans and will send the spirits of the Querent soaring, the message should be analyzed carefully lest the Querent put too much faith and dependence into the contents. Beware of a letdown unless prudence and caution are observed.

JACK—The Jack of Hearts is the card of romance. In the center of the spread the card defines a portion of the Querent's personality.

In the upper and lower wings, the card denotes a romantic interlude. If the Jack is an end card, a period of great happiness will come after many tests and trials. In any other position, the romance will surely be fleeting. The card warns against hedonism and excess of all kinds. If the Jack is in the inner corners of the wings, the Querent will meet a charming and vivacious person. But as with the other positions, this relationship will have no enduring value.

QUEEN—The Queen of Hearts is the Tarot Queen of Cups and implies all the same personality characteristics. Her positions have the same meanings as the positions of the other Queens and Kings.

KING—The King of Hearts is the Tarot King of Cups. His positions have the same meanings as the positions of the other Kings and Queens. A King of Hearts personality may marry a Queen of Hearts personality and find happiness. This does not hold true in any other suit.

CHAPTER FIFTEEN

The Suit of Spades

ACE—This card represents force, power, strength, and the ability to change the course of one's life. In all the wings it denotes situations wherein the Querent must act with great strength to overcome obstacles and to succeed where others have come in his way. The card also denotes great changes that will come about in the Querent's life as a result of the application of this strength. In the center of the spread, the strength of the card is a part of the Querent's nature and should be directed for the good of others as well as building the Querent's own prestige.

TWO—This card, appearing in any of the wings, represents a minor stumbling block that will crop up in the Querent's path. The importance of this stumbling block is denoted by the surrounding cards. In the center of the spread, the block will have an immediate effect on the Querent's life and can be related to the important influences now acting on him.

THREE—This is the card of swift resolution to take action in a seemingly minor matter. In any position, the Reader should examine the best road that the Querent might follow. The hasty decision is not always for the best. The other cards in the wing should be of great assistance in discovering the nature of the situation and the outcome of the Querent's actions.

FOUR—In any position, this card denotes healing, recovery, a period of rest which will lead to strength of mind and body. It can also denote fresh beginnings and the end of worry and uncertainty.

FIVE—This is a card of separation. It could be change of employment, the breaking of old ties, a change of abode, or new patterns of life.

In the upper wings, the situation tells of a friend or associate who will be leaving the Querent's life. In the lower wings, the separation is incidental and not terribly important in a direct manner.

SIX—In any position, the card is one of fear and anxiety. The Querent will find himself in a position where he must wait for others to make a decision for him. The Reader should advise the Querent to prepare for the decision, no matter what it may be, by planning alternate courses of action so that he will know what he must do for himself in any event.

SEVEN—In any position this card means partial fulfillment of one's plans. There will be setbacks but the goal can be achieved. It is also possible that the Querent is disappointed in the outcome of a project. The other cards in the wing should offer advice and conclusions for any of these matters.

EIGHT—In any position, this card denotes contentment. The other cards surrounding the Eight should be examined to see where this happy force is coming from.

NINE—The card has a meaning similar to the Tower of the Tarot. It denotes great changes, purges, and the end of worn-out, unnecessary, and detrimental forces in the Querent's life. If it is in the left-hand wings, there is an indication that the Querent may accept these changes to better his life or to maintain his present course.

TEN—The card denotes a wall or barrier that must be overcome. This can be opposition of any kind. Found in any of the wings and especially as the end card to a wing, the Ten is best considered as a warning to examine the cause of the wall. Clues for the best way to overcome the obstacles may be found by studying neighboring cards.

If the upper left-hand wing ends with this card, it is best to follow the natural course. If the right wing ends with this card, the alternate wing should be examined.

JACK—If this card faces a Heart or a Club, it represents a person of the sex opposite to the Querent's. If the Jack of Spades faces a Spade or a Diamond, it represents a member of the Querent's own sex. If it falls as an end card, determine sex by the direction in which the eyes face. The Jack represents the Tarot Knight and Page of Swords. The applicable sex should be determined and then a study of the Tarot delineation of character examined. To obtain the meaning of positions, of the Jack in the spread, apply the position rules governing the Kings and Queens of all suits.

QUEEN—The card is the same as the Tarot Queen of Swords. The positions of the card in the spread have the same meanings for divination as the positions of the other Queens. Because of her intuitive powers and sharpness of mind, this woman can be a valuable friend or a dire enemy.

KING—The King of Spades is the Tarot King of Swords. The same rules of placement in the spread apply here as in the other suits (see Tarot text).

Divination with an ordinary deck is a fascinating and an adequate substitute when no Tarot cards are available.

Because the Tarot includes astrology and numerology as a part of the procedure of divination, it is now necessary to offer a brief explanation of the way these two branches of knowledge can be applied to a reading either of the Tarot or of the standard deck of playing cards.

CHAPTER SIXTEEN

Astrology, Numerology, and the Tarot

When reading a spread, it is necessary to have all the available information about the personality of the Court cards and also to find a method for deciding when the predictions will occur. The gypsies gave an astrological significance to the Court cards and, by examining the numbers on the cards, it was possible for them to decide the day, month, week, and year that the prediction would take place.

People who use the cards every day may use the system of "mystical addition" to decide upon the number corresponding to the particular date and then they search out the card representing that day in the Tarot spread. If the card that bears the number of the day appears in the spread, the events will happen immediately; if it does not appear, the predicted events will take longer to occur.

To begin, let's outline the associations of the Tarot cards that bear these astrological interpretations.

The Suit of Cups—the planet Mars; strength, power, the masculine principle.

KING—the sign of Aries.
QUEEN—the sign of Taurus.
KNIGHT—the sign of Capricorn.
PAGE—the sign of Gemini.

The Suit of Wands—the sun and Jupiter; strength, warmth, benevolence, power of good.

KING—the sign of Libra.
QUEEN—the sign of Scorpio.
KNIGHT—the sign of Pisces.
PAGE—the sign of Sagittarius.

The Suit of Swords—Saturn and Mercury; age, authority, intelligence.

KING—the sign of Libra.
QUEEN—the sign of Virgo.
KNIGHT—the sign of Leo.
PAGE—the sign of Cancer.

The Suit of Pentacles—Venus and the moon; love of beauty, feminine principle, the cycles of the moon affect emotions.

KING—Taurus.
QUEEN—Sagittarius.
KNIGHT—Aries.
PAGE—Aquarius.

Where ever these Court cards may fall in a spread, they retain their astrological significance.

Any good astrology book can give you the delineation of character in the signs of the Zodiac. Certain signs are more compatible with some signs than with others. This understanding of the character of the people represented by the Court cards can give further information in such problems as divorce and arguments; such understanding gives insight into jealousy, shyness, and the other personal traits that continually pop up in an analysis of the character of a Court card. When there are problems between man and woman, it is quite sure that the comparison of personality according to the Zodiac will give the explanation clearly.

The seasons of the year are denoted by the *Aces* of the different suits when they appear in the spread.

The Ace of Cups—spring.

The Ace of Wands—autumn.

The Ace of Swords—summer.

The Ace of Pentacles—winter.

With this information, the reading of a spread may be more definite. It is possible, once the season is known, to understand when something will, or did, happen.

The science of numerology can contribute a lot to reading the cards. The type of addition used is simple enough to understand. To get the number of a specific day, do the following:

Month + Date + Year = Number

Example:

August 30, 1937

August is the 8th month, so August becomes the number 8.

The date $30 = 3 + 0 = 3$

The year $1937 = 1 + 9 + 3 + 7 = 20 = 2 + 0 = 2$

Now add together the $8 + 3 + 2 = 13 = 1 + 3 = 4$

So, the number for August 30, 1937 is 4. That day was a 4 day.

This can be done with any day of the week, any year. Take today's date and add it together this way. Say it comes out to the number 5. The fifth card of the Tarot pack is the Hierophant. There is a 5 in each suit of the Tarot. Pull these cards from the pack and examine them. When you are reading every day and any of the cards numbered 5 show up, on a 5 day of course, the future will come to pass immediately. It is also interesting to note that on a 5 day it is more than likely that you will encounter situations and people similar to the interpretations of the 5 cards of the suits and the Trump number 5. Try it! On a 4 day, check all the 4's in the pack and remember their meanings. See if the day doesn't seem to work out along those lines! If more than one number 4 card appears in the spread, the prophecy of both 4 cards will occur that day.

In numerology with cards we never exceed the number 9. It won't work! If the day adds up to, say, 28, $2 + 8 = 10$, we never work with two digits so 10 becomes $1 + 0 = 1$. There are number 10 cards in the Tarot deck and, for that matter, the Tarot has cards for any day that adds up to a number under twenty-two. But for the most accuracy, it is wise to break the number into one digit first. Then you may want to check the two-digit number against the similarly marked Tarot card as a supplementary reading.

When using these methods of clarification in reading a spread, the *last* card in the spread is the key to forecasting time. Let us assume that you have laid out a spread that ends with the Ace of Cups. You will know by the presence of the Ace that the event predicted will happen in spring. If the Ace happens to fall in another position in the spread, it still means that an event happened in spring. If the card designating the immediate future—the number 6 card in the spread—is an Ace, the immediate future then changes to the forthcoming spring. If you are laying the spread out in winter, your future time is established by the presence of the Ace. To determine the day in spring, check the last card. Say it is the 5 of Wands. Then you now know that 5 weeks after the beginning of spring, on a day that adds up to the number 5, the prophecy of the 5 of Wands will come to pass.

Perhaps there is no Ace in the spread that is before you. You can still discover the time element involved by the last card, which denotes days, weeks, months, and years. You can also find the number of the day on which the event will occur. Should the last card be a Court card, just keep going backward until you find the closest number card to the last card in the spread. Your time element will then become clear. Should that last card with a number on it be the 6 of Pentacles, and you are aware that the Querent has been waiting for something to occur for about 6 years, you may then inform the Querent that the event will happen very shortly, on a day that adds up to 6. If the event involved will surely take many years to come to pass, say the completion of an involved project like a book—see how long the project has been under way and advise the Querent that at the end of a period of 6 years, including the time already passed, on a day that adds up to 6, the project will be completed.

It may seem that the Querent must wait a very long time for the completion of his desires. There is always a good reason for this. It is likely that the Querent is not emotionally ready to accept the new responsibility or does not have enough experience behind him to successfully accomplish his goal. The Querent should be in-

148

formed that this period of waiting is for his benefit. Many things will occur between the present and the time denoted by the suit and number of the last card. The Querent will learn much during this waiting period and, when the happening finally does occur, he will be in a position to receive the maximum benefit from the situation.

The Querent may feel that the time factor involved is too long or seems too far into the future to wait for with patience. If this is the case, it is wise to advise the Querent that good things often take a long time to happen. If the Querent does not want to endure so much waiting, chances are that the goal is not that important to him. He may think so at the moment but, if he is not willing to "wait it out," he really does not want it badly. In such a case, alternate routes for the future should be discussed by examining the other cards in the spread.

It is a good idea to adopt the habit of adding up the date of each day as it goes by. In this way, you will be able to anticipate what each day will bring, because you know the meaning of the cards in the Tarot pack that correspond to the number of that particular day. Invariably, you will find that circumstances repeat themselves on days that add up to the same number. On 2 days, the romantic part of your life will usually come to the fore. On 5 days, you will usually encounter situations pertaining to religion, the church, and the established moral codes of society. On a 7 day, you will usually encounter situations related to gain and finances. With an understanding of the Tarot and a basic education in the mechanics of mystical addition, the future is never a real mystery.

We have already learned how to tell days, weeks, months, and years by the suit of the cards. The number at the top of the card is also vitally important. Check the date that you are laying out the spread. Does it correspond to the digit or digits at the top of the last card? If it does and you feel that the future will come about shortly, it could be today! Should the last card bear two numbers, break them down to one number by adding them together until you obtain one digit. This will tell you how many days, weeks, months, and years are involved, depending, again, on the suit.

As this short study denotes, there are many ways to perfect your reading of the cards. The Reader must be many things; above all, he must be a bit of a psychologist. We will discuss, in the last chapter, the most important things to be remembered when reading the cards.

CHAPTER SEVENTEEN

Things to Remember

The person who choses to become a reader of cards—whether Tarot or standard playing cards—must never forget or shun one thing: the Reader's responsibility to the Querent.

There is nothing more powerful than suggestion. In divination with cards, suggestion plays the most important role. The Querent is anxious to learn how a situation will turn out. Some people will grasp at straws to insure happiness. Here is where your responsibility comes in. Whatever you tell the Querent must be for his growth and his understanding of himself and others. It is the Reader's responsibility to direct the Querent in the proper direction to achieve his goals. The messages in the cards are the road-markers on this path.

An excellent example of irresponsible action on the part of a card reader is shown in an incident that occurred just a few years ago. A dear friend of mine went to a card reader to find out about her future. The woman told her quite accurately what she had encountered in the past and then told her with equal conviction what was coming. She predicted a divorce, sickness, and possibly death. This was the worst thing she could have done. Giving no further insight to the problems surrounding this unhappiness, she closed her reading with a warning to be careful of travel by plane and to watch for signs of infidelity.

My friend came home hysterical. She began to imagine that her husband, who often worked late at the office, was cheating on her. She began to notice every ache and pain as though they were symptoms of a grave illness about to beset her. While driving to her friends' home, she became so aware of danger that, instead of being more careful on the road, she was preoccupied with thoughts of an accident. When a plane flew low over the road, she became panicky and lost control of the car, sending it into a tree. Fortunately, she was not seriously hurt.

When such things do show up in the cards, modify them and if the Querent seems to be the nervous, anxious type, always worrying and constantly afraid, it would be best to ignore that part of the reading. Instead, give sound advice directed toward the way that the Querent should act, if, in the distant future, any situations of this nature should arise. The suggestion that these things will happen and bring disaster, should be avoided scrupulously.

The prophecy of death should never, under any circumstances, be disclosed. The suggestion of death could easily contribute to the actual death of a person who, under normal conditions, would have led a long and happy life. When we believe we are going to die, we actually court death, perhaps not even realizing it.

The cards are always accurate, but interpretation varies with experience. When you reach a stumbling block in your reading—anything that could hurt the Querent's feelings or cause him to act on a suggestion that could lead to disaster—it is always best to avoid the actual reading and to offer advice should the occasion arise in *someone else's* life. The general wisdom of the Tarot is for all people and can be applied to all human situations.

It is possible for the wise Reader to help the Querent overcome some problem that may show up in the spread. While it is not wise to tell a person that he or she will encounter grave financial setbacks or any other unhappiness that will affect his or her emotional stability, the Reader can advise ways to *avoid* trouble. If one of these tragic situations turns up in the spread, it is necessary first to examine the other cards to determine the cause of the problem. Then the Reader can direct the Querent away from the source of the problem, using the wisdom of the Tarot and, thus, possibly alter the events to come or, at least, soften the impact.

Perhaps a reading shows that the Querent will enter into a divorce. The Reader should examine the causes leading up to the happening. It can be discussed with the Querent in such a manner that the actual divorce is not foretold; rather, the Querent can be advised of ways to improve his or her marriage according to the messages in the cards, so that the future will be happier for all concerned. Should the divorce still occur, at least the Reader cannot carry the responsibility for having given the suggestion of a divorce to the Querent. There are some marriages that are fated for disaster, no matter what anyone does. At least the Querent will have done his best to try to save the marriage and the Reader will not have shirked his or her responsibility to the Querent.

Often the card of Death shows up in a spread. In the ordinary deck of playing cards there is no Death card. In a Tarot reading, the Death card is number thirteen. Should this card occur, the Reader *should not*, under any circumstances, read or interpret this card to mean actual death. The Querent should be advised that a change is coming in his life that will bring new surroundings, new people, and new opportunities. The Death card is a card of *rebirth*, never one of actual death. The Reader must be cautious when discussing any fear that may dwell in the Querent. The wisdom of the Tarot has a solution for all problems and especially fear. Man's greatest fear is loss, whether it be loss of life or loss of possessions or the loss of love. The gypsies, in their great understanding of life—so well described in their analysis of the Tarot—explain that loss occurs to make room for new gain. They believe that death is a beginning of a new life, never the complete end. The loss of love makes way for a newer and stronger love. Loss of a valued possession makes room for the receipt of a new and more valuable article to take its place. When we find something leaving our lives it is because we no longer really need it. This is hard to believe at first, but with the passage of time the proof of this wisdom is shown. When fear exists it is time to examine ourselves and to understand why we are afraid. The woman afraid to be left in seclusion, cannot, apparently, rely on her own strength and understanding to calm her. Rather than brood over fear, the message of the Tarot is to face that fear and call it by its name. Once the problem crawls out of the shadowed retreat of the mind into the light, it can no longer be something to be afraid of. The reader should advise this woman to discuss this fear with her husband tactfully and then to act on the results of the discussion. Once a positive action is taken in a negative situation—and a fear is about as negative as you can get—the problem dissolves and growth is accomplished. As the wisdom of the Tarot preaches, one positive action leads to another until a succession of these positive actions bears fruit and a new cycle of growth begins.

The entire Tarot is "a little bit of this and a little bit of that" all making for a perfectly balanced conception of what life, and of course people, really are all about. The future as presented by the Tarot is never black and white. We are given an insight into what will come and also the knowledge to make the very best of it for ourselves and for the other people involved. Everything is subject to change by the hand of man. Knowing yourself helps to change things or change your understanding for your own gain.

It is necesasry to stress one important point. The cards, whether Tarot or ordinary playing cards, should never be used for monetary gain. To receive personal profit from a reading of the cards is, according to Tarot scholar Wenzell Brown, "to debase the ancient, mystical symbols of the cards." Also, from a more practical point of view it is dangerous, for many cities have ordinances against forecasting the future if money changes hands. Reading the cards is a responsibility. You must always remember that people's joys and sorrows, their past and present are their most precious possessions. Your responsibility is to give insight and wise advice about the future. If you should be tempted to change a reading for your own personal gain, whether to gain the affections of the Querent or his gratitude in the form of gifts or actions, you are placing yourself at the mercy of the power within the cards. This power will eventually turn against you and bring you misery. If the cards are used for good and to help others, you will be rewarded by the happiness you will have given. By helping someone else, you will learn much about yourself and your own dilemmas. The cards are meant to teach wisdom to the Querent and to the Reader. If this mission is accomplished, both parties benefit.